Recommendations

Robert's book is one of the best books I have read on the person and partnership of the Holy Spirit. This book is very thorough and will be a great help to any who want to know God the Holy Spirit and how He is carrying out the ministry of Jesus through believers today. This is a must-read for any who want to be used in healing ministry or have the present-day ministry of Holy Spirit working in their life. Robert's use of the scripture and experience to back it up makes this book a great read!

— Mark Anderson
Evangelist, Author, and Singer

It has been my privilege to see Robert grow and mature as a devoted disciple of Jesus Christ, from his early days of salvation to his call to minister in the nations. This book was not birthed from the ivory towers of academia, but rather from the trenches of real-life experience. His passion for Jesus Christ and His Kingdom coming and His will being done on earth as it is in Heaven pours out through the pages of this book. I pray you will encounter the fullness of God as you read!

— Phillip O'Reilly
Senior Pastor, The Rock of KC Church

Brother Robert is a true seeker of the presence of the Lord. In his book, he has simplified profound mysteries of the Holy Spirit, helping believers pursue the experience of His presence, rather than just the theory of His person. This book is detailed, yet comprehensive—an overflow of the author's intimate walk with the Holy Spirit.

— Sachin Gupta
Pastor, New Life Church, India

I joyfully recommend this book to any church desiring to enter fully into the realm of the Holy Spirit. With practical wisdom and insight, Robert speaks of the glorious dimensions of the doctrine of the Holy Spirit. He puts a strong emphasis on developing intimate relationship with Holy Spirit, which many writers have missed. Knowing Robert and working alongside him, I know this book has come out of his various encounters with Holy Spirit.

— Bachitter Singh
Senior Pastor, Baptist church Abohar, India

THE FATHER'S PROMISE

THE FATHER'S PROMISE

ROBERT PRAKASH

Dedication

I am dedicating this book to my spiritual father, mentor, and dear friend, Ben Baird. I am forever indebted to you for your patience, kindness, love, and discipline. From the early days of walking with Jesus until this day, your care, concern, prayers, love, and faith in me have been the pillars that kept me strong.

Since the beginning of knowing you and learning from you, I have been amazed how you have denied yourself and chose to give me opportunity upon opportunity so that I can grow and become all that God has destined for me. You never sought to mold me according to your own expectations, but rather your continual loving encouragement caused me to find the specific path God designed for my life.

I couldn't imagine my spiritual life without you. This book is a direct product of your discipleship in my life. I love you so much!

Robert Prakash

Acknowledgments

Special thanks to Jesus, my Lord, Savior, and Lover, who loved and accepted me when I was beyond hopeless and helpless. I am amazed that You chose me to represent You in my weaknesses and imperfections. You truly are Amazing Grace.

Special thanks to my wonderful wife, Abhilasha. Your presence, love, patience, kindness, and selflessness has been the second greatest blessing in my life. I thank God for the special gift you are to me. Without your help, input, and advice, this book would be incomplete.

Special thanks to Sue Baird, Sharon Stark, and L'auren Aspenlieder for reviewing and editing this book. You have played such an integral part, for which I am thankful.

Special thanks to Pastor Phillip and Susan O'Reilly. Your leadership, example, love, and care have been so significant. Thank you for believing in me and standing with me.

Contents

Forward

I have known Robert since he first became a follower of Jesus as a teenager. I liked him immediately. He communicated clearly to me one thing: He was willing to be different. Not just for the idea of being different, but for the sake of the Kingdom of God. In my own life, the person of the Holy Spirit became extremely important early in my Christian walk. Compassion was one of the gifts the Lord gave me, and I discovered how partnering with the Holy Spirit gave me the ability, discernment, and wisdom to minister to many through this gifting and various other gifts of the Holy Spirit. Many teachers have poured their wisdom and knowledge of the Holy Spirit into me, and I am indebted to them, but I'm most grateful to the Lord Jesus Christ and the ability for me to have a friendship with the Holy Spirit. I cannot begin to convey the great influence the Holy Spirit has been in my life.

Robert is both informed in the Word of God and very passionate about the work of the Gospel of Jesus Christ. He is a dynamic communicator, yet very determined to be factual. He desires, in both spoken and written communication, to always be clear, concise, and truthful.

I am honored to know Robert as a spiritual father, a friend, and a co-laborer. I highly recommend this book to anyone wanting to know the person of the Holy Spirit. It will empower, inspire, equip, and activate you. This book is full of graphic and bold illustrations that clearly show God's Word brought to life in our present day. As you read, you will be challenged to a deeper, more intimate walk with Jesus. It will awaken you to the possibility of greater realization and revelation of the person and power of the Holy Spirit in your own life. If you want "more" of God, this book is for you.

Ben Baird
Retired Pastor, The Rock of KC Church

Introduction

A GLIMPSE INTO THE SUPERNATURAL

Stories of miracles, face-to-face encounters with God, and the impossible becoming reality pierced the subconscious unbelief of my heart, and my spirit began to yearn. A yearning that surpassed any physical urge and transcended every soulish desire. A yearning that erupted from the spirit, shaking the very core of my being. Many would scoff and say these stories and encounters were just dramatized lies. But I did not have to question if these testimonies were true, for the spirit within me was weeping and bearing witness. Tears began to roll down my face as a new horizon of hope shone in my heart.

I was scated in a hall with 400 others, quietly listening to the preacher. But on the inside, my spirit was raging. Like a wild animal locked in a cage, howling and fighting for freedom. So was my spirit crying out for the reality of what I was hearing. Though I appeared calm, I was screaming so loudly on the inside that I could not give all my attention to the message. A cry flowed from the inside:

Lord, I want this anointing, presence, and power! I need it, Lord! I don't want to live another day without it. Lord, I must have it!

This desperate cry was beyond normal prayer. It surpassed all my logic and reasoning. It was a cry not from my mind or soul, but from the depths of my spirit. It was a cry that moved my entire being, as an earthquake levels cities.

The desire in me raged so strongly that I began to feel frightened. I felt compelled to stand up and scream out, to give voice to what was burning inside of me. After the message, there was a break time before the next session. When everyone else began to leave the hall, I laid down and began to weep on the floor. Though no one really knew what was happening in me, the Lord knew. For His attention is upon the contrite, the broken in spirit (Isaiah 57:15). Tears continued to fall as small puddles formed on the floor. I resolved in my heart that I could not leave this conference without satisfying my spirit's cry.

Can the Holy Spirit so consume someone that the very works of Jesus flow effortlessly through their lives? Is it possible to see untold numbers of the blind seeing, deaf hearing, and crippled walking? Can the God we know, who often feels so distant and impersonal, manifest Himself so powerfully in us that we are changed in a moment? I knew God was no respecter of persons. If He did it for one, He would do it for me. The question is not, *Will the Holy Spirit fall on me?* But rather, *Does my hunger and desperation rightly represent the immeasurable value of His presence?*

Randy Clark, a world famous preacher and teacher, returned to share one more message that evening. He began by saying that God gives drink to the thirsty. Are we thirsty for Him? Blessed are those who hunger and thirst for righteousness, for they will be satisfied (Matthew 5:6). There is physical hunger. There is emotional hunger. But, there is also spiritual hunger. This spiritual hunger, when birthed by the Holy Spirit, is a dangerous reality. Maintaining spiritual hunger is an open door into the supernatural. If you have to ask, *Am I hungry?*, then you probably are not. I don't need to ask if I feel physically hunger. Why? Because I can feel it.

Randy Clark shared testimony after testimony, how God raised up Heidi Baker and many others who are now changing nations and regions for God's glory. Then came the time for impartation—to invite the One who burns with an eternal flame to make us ministers of His fire.

Though I was in a strong season of hunger and desperation that had lasted many months, still I was unsure how to practically obtain it by myself. I read books, meditated on the Word, and spent hours crying out to God for more, but still I felt like the Eunuch who replied to Philip, *How can I, unless someone guides me?* (Acts 8:30–31).

The Lightnings of Heaven

After the message, Randy gave these instructions, "We will pray for everyone, but first, we want to minister to those the Holy Spirit touches first. If you feel electricity flowing in your head, shoulders, arms, and hands, or you are overcome by His presence or feel a fire, I want these people to come up to the front first."

The moment Randy invited the Holy Spirit to come, I felt a strange current begin to flow into my body. My shoulders, arms, hands, and even my legs and feet began to shake as power was flowing into me. It was a strange feeling. Prior to this event, I had felt many forms of the presence of God, such as His overwhelming love that caused me to weep or see a vision. This time, a tangible power was flowing in and through me. Though I felt that I could choose to resist it to a degree and try to stop shaking, I didn't want to. I wanted Him so deeply that I didn't care how He chose to come upon me. Any manifestation was fine as long as I got Him.

After a moment, Randy said, "If the presence and power of God is touching you as I said, come forward now." I tried to walk up to the front, near the church altar, but it was difficult for me because of the extreme shaking. I was doing shutter-steps toward the front. When I was about 15–20 feet from Randy, he stretched out his hand toward me and yelled something that I am not able to remember.

I was not ready for what was about to happen. Who could be ready for the lightning of heaven? How can a mortal body bear the weighty glory of God? The moment Randy pointed to me, an invisible power hit me with incredible force, sending me flying in the air. I hit the ground, and the waves of electricity magnified. My body was shaking so hard that it felt difficult to breathe. My hands were a blur from the intense speed of it. Before this encounter, I was crying out, saying, *More, Lord! More! I must have more!* But, during this time, I began to think, *Oh my, this is intense! Can I even bear it?* My legs and feet were shaking so hard that my shoes flew off my feet and landed several feet away from me.

I had no idea what I was really asking for. All I knew is that I wanted Him. I wanted that precious person called the Holy Spirit to be a living reality in my life. I know, theologically, that I have the Holy Spirit within me. But theology was not enough; I had to have the experience. Everything else seemed meaningless and empty. Life without Him is like Indian food without masala (spices). He means everything to me.

As I continued to lay on the floor, helpless to do anything but shake uncontrollably, my entire shirt became soaked in sweat. The hall was sufficiently air-conditioned, but the power inside of me was like a fire. I looked anything but peaceful: yelling, shaking, soaked in sweat, and gasping for breath. Though my body looked like a mess, I was very peaceful on the inside. Like a hurricane churning the ocean waves was my body, but directly under the ocean, the peaceful still waters were like my spirit. My spirit was calm and at peace.

The power and the shaking didn't stop. My body began to hurt, and my joints began to ache. Why? Was God trying to hurt me? At this point, I started to worry and began to cry out when I had a chance, in between gasping for air, *Lord! No more! I can't take anymore!* But, He knew what I could handle. People sometimes ask why people fall over, shake, or sweat profusely when the Holy Spirit manifests Himself. My practical answer to that question is this: A fallen, mortal body just can't handle all that heavy glory. If He came in the fullness of His glory, we would be no more. A mortal body just cannot respond perfectly to the weight of glory.

The waves of power seemed to become less at times, with less shaking, and yet at other times they would intensify. After 30–40 minutes of shaking helplessly on the floor, the Lord came to me in several visions and began to speak to me about His love and compassion for the nations. I have noticed and experienced that each time God endues me with power, He always imparts His heart of compassion. It's important to understand that compassion without power is helplessness, but power without compassion is selfishness and the glory of man. These two, power and compassion, are the double-edged sword of the Spirit.

> *Compassion without power is helplessness, but power without compassion is selfishness and the glory of man. These two, power and compassion, are the double-edged sword of the Spirit.*

After about 50 minutes, the power and shaking ceased. I continued to lay on the floor, traumatized by the power of God. I thought, *Well, I believe I got what I was asking for!* If this was a real encounter of His presence, then it must bear fruit. I love encounters with God and treasure them, but if there is not a change from that encounter, I question how much of it was actually God.

THE IMPOSSIBLE BECOMING NORMAL

From that time, I began to take risks of faith, attempting to do things that I normally would not have been willing and bold enough to do. I was invited to Miraz, Maharashtra, for a three-day healing meeting. The first day, a crowd of about 300 people came. God showed up and did many miracles.

The second day of the meeting, we were free until evening, so a believer friend invited us to his home for lunch. As we traveled to his house, I was sitting in the back of an old van. The shocks of the vehicle were in bad condition, and we were bouncing along. I wasn't in a mode of prayer or trying to be spiritual; I was just looking out the window. When we took a side road from the main highway, I noticed two men sitting on the highway divider. The highway divider was about six feet wide, covered in grass, and there were three small trees on it. The moment I saw them, the Holy Spirit jumped inside of me, and I could feel His excitement. Out of the corner of my eye, I caught one of the men making a hand gesture to the other.

At that moment, I jumped out of my seat and yelled, "Stop! Stop!!!" The driver became frightened at the intensity of my voice and immediately hit the brake. With a screeching sound, the van stopped at the edge of the road. "What happened?" The driver asked. I turned to my friend, Stavan, who was sitting next to me and said, "I think one of those guys is deaf. I want to pray for him."

We exited the van and walked across the street. The two men, about the ages of 27 and 28, were staring at us. Once we reached them, I asked if I could pray for anyone who is deaf or hard of hearing. They both pointed to their ears, then to their mouths, and shook their hands at us. Not understanding what they were trying to say, I repeated my question. They again responded with the same action. Stavan looked at me and said, "They are both deaf mutes; they can't hear or speak."

Full of excitement, I made hand gestures and tried to explain that I wanted to pray for them. They didn't understand. So, I proceeded to put my fingers in one of the deaf-mute's ears. He looked puzzled at what I was trying to do.

Then I prayed, "In Jesus' name, I command this generational curse of deafness to break! Deaf spirit, come out of him now!" I immediately pulled out my fingers and then began making snapping sounds next to his ears. To his surprise, he could hear and nodded his head in response to each snap. I snapped my fingers further and further away and he continued to signal that he could hear. Then suddenly a bus drove by honking the horn. The man was frightened at the loud sound! I thought, *No wonder these guys are sitting on this noisy highway divider! They are deaf!*

I then put my hand upon his mouth and commanded the mute spirit to leave him. After prayer, I looked at him and said, "Mama, papa!" He repeated the same clearly. Then I counted, *5...6...7...8...9 ...10...11...12*, and he repeated each word clearly. It was so exciting!

I then turned toward his friend who was in awe, seeing his friend able to hear and speak. Then I said, "It's your turn now!" I put my fingers in his ears and prayed the same thing. Upon testing his hearing by snapping my fingers, he made hand gestures that he could not hear anything. I again put my fingers in his ears and prayed, "You deaf spirit, come out of him now! I break this curse! Deaf ears open and hear!" I proceeded to snap my fingers again, but to no avail. He was still completely deaf.

Here is where most believers lose their faith and confidence. Satan is right there to give excuses for why the deaf person is not hearing. Many may say, *Oh, it is probably not God's will, and therefore he is not being healed.* Or another may think, *This is probably a really strong demon and we need to fast and pray before we can cast it out!* Or another may say, *This deafness may be the specific cross that God has given to this man to bear!* All of these thoughts are just excuses not to persevere in faith. Did God anoint me? Is it His will to heal all? Is the Holy Spirit upon me for the work of the Gospel? The answer to those three questions is definitely *yes!*

I then, for the third time, put my fingers in his ears and prayed, "You devil! I commanded you to come out, and I stand by that command! Get out of him now! Deaf ears, open now in Jesus's name! "This time, his ears immediately opened. You can recognize when a person born deaf starts hearing. You can see it on their face and in their eyes. After praying for his tongue, he began to speak clearly.

Though they started to hear and speak for the first time, they could not understand the sounds they were hearing. I wanted to tell them that Jesus healed them. After trying to explain through hand gestures, Stavan came to know that they went to a special school where deaf-mutes learn to read and write. We wrote on a paper: Can you come to the evening meeting? It is not too far from here. We want to give you a Bible. It is about God, Jesus, who healed you.

Their reply was so precious. They wrote: We definitely will come to receive this Bible. But can we bring all of our deaf-mute friends with us?

That evening, several more deaf-mutes began to speak and hear. It was a wonderful time. During those three days, the blind saw, the deaf heard, the mute spoke, and many with various afflictions were healed by the power of the Holy Spirit. Isn't He precious? That beautiful Holy Spirit? He was the one who did all this to glorify the name of Jesus (John 16:14).

On another occasion, I was invited to Unnao, Uttar Pradesh, for another three-day healing meeting. After preaching the Gospel and praying for a hundred sick people, we began to close the meeting. Then, a woman came up to me who sounded desperate. "Can you pray for my son?" she asked. I saw a local church volunteer carrying a boy in his arms, coming toward me. I could see that this child was crippled. The boy's name was Aazad, which means "freedom" in Urdu. But Aazad was anything but "free." I had the boy sit on the end of the stage. After asking his mother several questions, I found out that Aazad was ten years old and was born with crippled, deformed feet. He had never walked or even stood by himself.

I knelt down and took both of his deformed feet into my hands and began to pray, "You spirit of infirmity, in Jesus's name, I curse you, bind you, and command you to leave, and I break your power over this boy's feet! Healing power, resurrection power, flow into these feet and ankles now!" After praying a short prayer, I opened my eyes, but there was no difference whatsoever after my prayer. I took one foot into my hands and tried to bend them to a straight position in which, maybe, the boy could stand by himself. But, after applying much pressure, I quickly realized that the boy didn't have a functional ankle. The feet and ankles were twisted and in no way could be made straight.

I continued to act in faith by trying to have the boy stand or walk with our assistance, but it was no use. There was no way he could ever stand in that condition. After some more prayer, I gave him over to his mother and said, "I prayed in faith and I am believing for him to be healed. This is the first day of the healing meeting. If he needs more prayer, you can bring him the next two days."

> *Looking up into his mother's eyes, he said, "Look, mom! I can walk!"*

This was the first time she had heard about Jesus, and she lived about two hours away in a village. She picked up her boy and started on her long travel back.

Upon reaching her home, she placed Aazad on the bed and went to the kitchen to start cooking some food, for it was long past lunch time. After about 10–15 minutes, she heard Aazad yell loudly, Mommy! Mommy! Come here quickly! Worried, she ran to the doorway to see what happened. As she turned the corner and looked, Aazad also looked up at her. One hand was holding the side of the bed, and the other hand was in the air for balance, and he was taking several steps slowly. Looking up into his mother's eyes, he said, "Look mom! I can walk!"

I didn't know what had happened. We arrived late on the second day of the healing meeting. Upon reaching the meeting, we saw Aazad and his mom standing up in front of about 400 people. She was weeping and crying so strongly that it was too difficult for me to understand what she was saying. Abhilasha, my wife, who is fluent in the local dialect, began to explain to me what happened. Then it hit me, "Oh my! This is the boy!" We came up and interviewed them. I examined Aazad's feet, and they were perfect! There was no deformation; the ankle was perfectly healed and flexible. From a medical perspective, this is mind-blowing. God recreated joints, bone, tendons, ligaments, and muscle tissue within a moment of time. She shared how she spent much money on doctors and physical therapy and it did not help at all, but Jesus healed her son. That was their first experience of "church," and that is how church should be for everyone who comes! They now believe in Jesus and attend church regularly.

I could share story after story of the blind seeing, the deaf hearing, and many demonized people becoming free through the presence and power of the Holy Spirit. These two testimonies are written just to whet your appetite for the person of the Holy Spirit. The greatest testimony I can share, however, is not the crippled walking and tumors dissolving, but knowing this Holy Spirit personally. It is not His power that I want most, though it is important and necessary. It is His sweet presence and knowing His person that is the greatest treasure of all.

Again, I am not satisfied with my intimacy with Him; I want to know Him more and experience Him in a greater way. I want more of the anointing, presence, and power. My hunger continues for the only thing that can truly satisfy.

In the introduction of this book, I invite you into this pursuit with me. I will be teaching you most of what I know about the Holy Spirit, but this adventure of knowing Him will never end, because each day I come to know Him more and learn so much more about His ways. Let this book be a beginning point, and not an end, to knowing and experiencing this wonderful person called the Holy Spirit.

1

The Godhead and the HolySpirit

A Pure Heart

In this first chapter, we are going to focus upon three important points from Scripture pertaining to the Holy Spirit:

† Who is the Holy Spirit?

† What work has the Holy Spirit done in history, and what is He doing today?

† What is our personal relationship with the Holy Spirit?

Before starting, I want to both warn and encourage you. In John 5:39–40, Jesus said to the religious Jews, "You search the Scriptures, because you think that in them you have eternal life; and these are they which testify about me. Yet you will not come to me, that you may have life." (WEB)

There are many who approach Scripture to know about God, but they fail to know Him in a personal and experiential way that produces a living relationship. My goal in writing this book is not that we would know about the Holy Spirit, but that we would experience Him personally. If you are content with theological knowledge that lacks experience, beware, lest a Pharisaical spirit be found operating in you! You know you are on the right track if your heart yearns for the experience of what you are reading, and the experience is your goal. In this book, you will find basic, practical truth that will launch you into such experiences.

Who is this Holy Spirit?

We are going to look at a few scriptures concerning who the Holy Spirit is.

> Now when all the people were baptized, Jesus also had been baptized and was praying. The sky was opened, and the Holy Spirit descended in a bodily form like a dove on him; and a voice came out of the sky, saying, "You are my beloved Son. In You I am well pleased."
>
> — Luke 3:21–22

> I will pray to the Father, and he will give you another Counselor, that He may be with you forever.
>
> — John 14:16

> Go, and make disciples of all nations, baptizing them in the name of the Father and of the Son and of the Holy Spirit.
>
> — Matthew 28:19

> The grace of the Lord Jesus Christ, the love of God, and the fellowship of the Holy Spirit, be with you all. Amen.
>
> — 2 Corinthians 13:14

In each of these Scriptures, we can identify three different persons. We see Jesus, Father God, and the Holy Spirit. These are not isolated references, for the New Testament is filled with these three unique persons. We can basically understand from the Bible that

God is revealed as three distinct persons. We also have strong evidence from Scripture that there is only one God (Deuteronomy 6:4; James 2:19; Isaiah 43:10–11, 44:8). Many theologians have spent their entire lives trying to solve this intellectual issue of how one God can be expressed in three different persons.

Now we must accept this, not by reasoning, but by faith; there is only one God who is manifested in three distinct persons. But, the more important issue is not how we can accept it intellectually or theologically, but rather the question: How can we personally experience each person of the Godhead?

Many years ago, I used to read over these scriptures quickly. But now when I read them, I see an invitation. Do you see it? It is an invitation to know each person of the Godhead. I get excited when I read this. I can have a personal relationship not only with Jesus, but also with the Holy Spirit.

To explain the Godhead, I want to use the practical example of a family. For example, Rajendra Singh is married to Rekha Singh, and they have one son named Sunil Singh. Each member of this family has two names. A given name and a family name. In the same way, we can understand God as a family. Father God, Jesus the Son of God, and Holy Spirit God. Now if I want to know this family personally, I would need to spend time and fellowship with each member of the family.

Many people talk about their spiritual lives and refer to God only as God. If you have a deep, personal relationship with each unique member of the Godhead, then you won't refer to them as just God, but You will relate to them specifically. Do you know when the Holy Spirit is speaking to you? Can you distinguish the presence, voice, and person of the Father as compared to the Son and the Holy Spirit?

During prayer, ministry, or just fellowshipping with God, I can usually distinguish which member of the Godhead is speaking to me, and whose presence is being manifested at that time. Remember, I don't have a relationship with just the Singh family, but specifically with Rajendra, Rekha, and Sunil. They are different, unique, and separate, but yet they are still one. In the same way, the Father is unique, and so is Jesus and the Holy Spirit.

They all possess the same character, desires, motives, and nature, but they have different roles and different personalities. They are all holy, loving, and kind, but they have different roles and actions, though they are always working together for the same purpose. If you don't know God as three unique persons, then I want to encourage and excite you with this amazing reality you can live in!

Some people might oppose this teaching and say we only need to know God as one. Others teach so strongly that God is one that they neglect to know each member individually. Let's look at a few scriptures to see how unique and separate they are.

> Whoever speaks a word against the Son of Man, it will be forgiven him; but whoever speaks against the Holy Spirit, it will not be forgiven him, neither in this age, nor in that which is to come.
>
> — Matthew 12:32

In this verse, we can see a big difference between Jesus and the Holy Spirit. Clearly, they are different persons, and there is a unique consequence if we relate to the Holy Spirit in a specific sinful way. This consequence is not there in relationship to Jesus.

> Go, and make disciples of all nations, baptizing them in the name of the Father and of the Son and of the Holy Spirit.
>
> — Matthew 28:19

Why did Jesus command us to baptize believers in three unique names? What is a name? A name represents a person. Jesus commands us to baptize not just in the name of the Father or the Son, but also in the name of the Holy Spirit. Why? Would it not be sufficient to say, "Baptize them in name of God"? According to Jesus, it would not be sufficient. The Godhead is incomplete without the precious Holy Spirit. The three complete the Godhead.

> At the ninth hour, Jesus cried with a loud voice, saying, "Eloi, Eloi, lama sabachthani?" which is, being interpreted, "My God, my God, why have you forsaken me?"
>
> — Mark 15:34

Again, we see two distinct persons in the Godhead. Father God did not bear the sins of mankind, nor did He take on flesh to be crucified. The Father did not reject Himself, but His Son. It was Jesus who was rejected and forsaken by the Father in order to redeem mankind. God is not one person, but three separate persons.

The Bible is very specific about each person of the Godhead, because God wants us to know and value each individually. The scriptures clearly state that the Holy Spirit is God (Acts 5:3–4). The Holy Spirit is just as much God as the Father or Jesus, no more or no less.

Wherever I teach, I see a consistent problem. Most believers know Jesus very well, and they know about the Father, too, but very few people know about the Holy Spirit. Or, if they do, they have little idea who He really is. To most, He seems mystical and mysterious. They can understand Jesus easily, but the Holy Spirit is often misunderstood. That is the very reason I am writing this book—to make this wonderful, precious person known.

The Bible is very specific about each person of the Godhead, because God wants us to know and value each individually.

So, we started this teaching with the first question: Who is the Holy Spirit? Now, we can clearly see that the Holy Spirit is fully God, equal with the Father and the Son, the third member of the Godhead, and a unique person.

THE WORKS OF THE HOLY SPIRIT

We are now going to look into the second question: What work has the Holy Spirit done in history, and what is He doing today? The purpose of knowing this is to produce thankfulness of heart and give us a reason to worship and praise God. Also, if we know what works the Holy Spirit has done and what He does, our hearts are prepared for an encounter of His presence. Faith usually precedes experience. Knowing what He does produces faith, which allows us to perceive and encounter Him.

Creator

Consider the following verse:

> God said, "Let us make man in our image, after our likeness, and let them have dominion over the fish of the sea, and over the birds of the sky, and over the livestock, and over all the earth, and over every creeping thing that creeps on the earth." God created man in his own image. In God's image he created him; male and female he created them.
>
> — Genesis 1:26–27

This verse revealed the Godhead in the Old Testament. God said, Let Us make man... Creation was not the isolated work of the Father, nor the Son. Creation was a special work they did together. But what role did the Holy Spirit have in our creation?

> You send out your Spirit and they are created. You renew the face of the ground.
>
> — Psalm 104:30

The Spirit of God has made me, and the breath of the Almighty gives me life.

— Job 33:4

As we will see again and again in this study, it is the Holy Spirit who manifests and performs the work of God. The Father and the Son were involved in the planning and process of creation, but it was the Holy Spirit who created us.

One day, I was in prayer and the Holy Spirit started showing me visions of how God created man. I saw the moist soil of the earth, then special light, looking similar to lightning, carving out of the soil a human shaped body. Within a moment, the soil turned to human flesh. The transition from soil to flesh was so natural that it was stunning to behold. The lightning presence was not a special "power," but the actual person of the Holy Spirit. The Holy Spirit doesn't have a specific form, but He is often revealed and experienced as fire, electricity, and light.

Who was the precious One who created you and me? The Holy Spirit was the intimate One who formed us. The Father smiled and sent forth His Spirit, and Jesus was rejoicing over us as the Holy Spirit created us.

"…knowing this first, that no prophecy of Scripture is of private interpretation. For no prophecy ever came by the will of man: but holy men of God spoke, being moved by the Holy Spirit.

— 2 Peter 1:20–21

The Voice of God

The Holy Spirit is the voice of God. God communicates to us through His Spirit. Every book from Genesis to Revelation was inspired and written by the Holy Spirit. He is the author of the Bible. Let us look at a few more scriptures to establish this point.

> I heard the Lord's voice, saying, "Whom shall I send, and who will go for Us?" Then I said, "Here I am. Send me!" He said, "Go, and tell this people, 'You hear indeed, but don't understand; and you see indeed, but don't perceive.' Make the heart of this people fat. Make their ears heavy, and shut their eyes, lest they see with their eyes, and hear with their ears, and understand with their heart, and turn again, and be healed.
>
> — Isaiah 6:8–10

> When they didn't agree among themselves, they departed after Paul had spoken one word, "The Holy Spirit spoke rightly through Isaiah, the prophet, to our fathers, saying, 'Go to this people, and say, in hearing, you will hear, but will in no way understand. In seeing, you will see, but will in no way perceive. For this people's heart has grown callous. Their ears are dull of hearing. Their eyes they have closed. Lest they should see with their eyes, hear with their ears, understand with their heart, and would turn again, and I would heal them.
>
> — Acts 28:25–27

The prophet saw the Lord Jesus sitting on the throne (compare Isaiah 6:1–5 and John 12:39–41). He then heard the "voice of the Lord." How did the Lord Jesus speak to Isaiah? Holy Spirit understood what the Lord wanted to say, and He communicated Jesus' thoughts, emotions, and desires. Again, we see the Godhead in this verse, "...who will go for Us?" This fact that the Holy Spirit is the voice of God is established by the clear statement, "The Holy Spirit spoke rightly through Isaiah the prophet..."

There are a few times when the Father spoke directly to people (John 12:28-29) but this was rare. The people said they heard thunder when the Father spoke, and that is exactly how Job describes God's voice (Job 37:2–5). Other than these specific instances, it is the Holy Spirit who spoke to the prophets and speaks to us today, in a gentle and clear voice (Also compare Jeremiah 31:33 and Hebrews 10:15–16). Not only did He fashion us and create us, He is the one who speaks to us and communicates to us what the Father and Jesus want to say.

> Now the birth of Jesus Christ was like this; for after his mother, Mary, was engaged to Joseph, before they came together, she was found pregnant by the Holy Spirit.
>
> — Matthew 1:18

> The angel answered her, "The Holy Spirit will come on you, and the power of the Most High will overshadow you. Therefore also the holy one who is born from you will be called the Son of God.
>
> — Luke 1:35

The birth of Jesus was impossible apart from the presence and power of the Holy Spirit. The Father sent His Son to this world (John 3:16), but God is Spirit (John 4:24). So who created the flesh, the body of Jesus in Mary's womb? Not only did the Holy Spirit create us, He also created the very body of Jesus.

Holy Spirit in Jesus's Ministry

Let us now see what impact the Holy Spirit had upon Jesus' ministry. Consider the Scriptures on the following page.

...even Jesus of Nazareth, how God anointed him with the Holy Spirit and with power, who went about doing good and healing all who were oppressed by the devil, for God was with him.

— Acts 10:38

Now when all the people were baptized, Jesus also had been baptized, and was praying. The sky was opened, and the Holy Spirit descended in a bodily form like a dove on him; and a voice came out of the sky, saying "You are my beloved Son. In you I am well pleased."... Jesus returned in the power of the Spirit into Galilee, and news about him spread through all the surrounding area... "The Spirit of the Lord is on me, because he has anointed me to preach good news to the poor. He has sent me to heal the brokenhearted, to proclaim release to the captives, recovering of sight to the blind, to deliver those who are crushed.

— Luke 3:21–22, 4:14,18

Not only was the birth of Jesus a miracle conducted by the Holy Spirit, but also the entire ministry of Jesus was dependent upon Him. It was only after the Spirit came upon Jesus that He was able to perform any miracles. You can say that the miraculous ministry of Jesus was actually the ministry of the Holy Spirit flowing through the person of Jesus. We will discuss this in great detail in Chapter 3.

...how much more will the blood of Christ, who through the eternal Spirit offered himself without defect to God, cleanse your conscience from dead works to serve the living God?

— Hebrews 9:14

In this verse, we clearly see the Godhead and how they worked together to atone for the sins of mankind. Many people don't know the role of the Holy Spirit in Christ's sacrifice. It is clear that when Jesus became the offering for our sin and took upon Himself our punishments, the Father rejected Him. Jesus cried out, and for the first time called God "God" instead of "Father."

"My God, My God, why have You forsaken Me?" Though Jesus's relationship with the Father was severed for our sake, the Holy Spirit did not forsake Jesus on the cross. It was "through the eternal Spirit" that Jesus was able to offer Himself as the sacrifice for our sins. Jesus went into the Holy of Holies with His own blood by the presence, power, and person of the Holy Spirit to redeem mankind. Without the Holy Spirit, redemption for mankind was not possible. The Holy Spirit was faithfully with Jesus until the very end.

> But if the Spirit of him who raised up Jesus from the dead dwells in you, he who raised up Christ Jesus from the dead will also give life to your mortal bodies through his Spirit who dwells in you.
>
> — Romans 8:11

Who raised Jesus from the dead? It was the Holy Spirit that raised Jesus from the grave! We see in Scripture that it is the Father who commands and decrees, but it is the Holy Spirit who fulfills those decrees. The Father, Himself, did not raise Jesus from the dead. The Father sent the Holy Spirit to raise Jesus up, and the Holy Spirit is the One who will raise us from the dead! The Holy Spirit is the miracle of the entire life of Jesus Christ, from birth to resurrection. Everything was dependent upon and fulfilled by the Spirit of God. Do you see how precious He is? Is your heart flowing with thanksgiving and love for Him?

> When he has come, he will convict the world about sin, about righteousness, and about judgment; about sin, because they don't believe in me; about righteousness, because I am going to my Father, and you won't see me any more; about judgment, because the prince of this world has been judged.
>
> — John 16:8–11

Therefore I make known to you that no man speaking by God's Spirit says, "Jesus is accursed." No one can say, "Jesus is Lord," but by the Holy Spirit.

— 1 Corinthians 12:3

No one can know they are a sinner apart from the convicting work of the Holy Spirit. No one can spiritually understand what sin is without the Holy Spirit (1 Corinthians 2:14). No one can perceive or understand who Jesus is without the Holy Spirit. No one can believe in Jesus without the work of the Holy Spirit. No one can understand judgment and God's victory over Satan without the Holy Spirit. He is the source of all spiritual knowledge and truth. All truth we have received is by the Holy Spirit's grace. He opens the eyes and gives sight to the spiritually blind (1 John 2:11, 2 Corinthians 4:3–4). Without His enlightening work and power, the work of the cross was done in vain. With a thankful heart have you ever praised and worshiped the precious Holy Spirit for opening your eyes and giving you revelation and understanding? Without this precious work, neither you nor I could have ever believed, confessed, or repented.

Jesus answered him, "Most certainly, I tell you, unless one is born anew, he can't see God's Kingdom."... Jesus answered, "Most certainly I tell you, unless one is born of water and spirit, he can't enter into God's Kingdom! That which is born of the flesh is flesh. That which is born of the Spirit is spirit.

— John 3:3,5–6

...in whom you also, having heard the word of the truth, the Good News of your salvation—in whom, having also believed, you were sealed with the promised Holy Spirit, who is a pledge of our inheritance, to the redemption of God's own possession, to the praise of his glory.

— Ephesians 1:13–14

When we believed in Jesus, we realized we were born again by the Holy Spirit. He is the one who raised up our dead spirit and gave it new life (Ephesians 2:4–5). He is the One who created within us a new heart and a new spirit (Ezekiel 36:26–27). Not only that, but He is the seal upon us, the very seal that declares we are Jesus's purchased possession. Without this inner work of the Holy Spirit, no one could be born again. Do you remember the day that your life forever changed? Do you remember the moment you realized you were born again? That moment was the work of the Holy Spirit.

They went out and preached everywhere, the Lord working with them and confirming the word by the signs that followed. Amen.

— Mark 16:20

But you will receive power when the Holy Spirit has come upon you. You will be witnesses to me in Jerusalem, in all Judea and Samaria, and to the uttermost parts of the earth."

— Acts 1:8

Now there are various kinds of gifts, but the same Spirit... But to each one is given the manifestation of the Spirit for the profit of all. For to one is given through the Spirit the word of wisdom, and to another the word of knowledge, according to the same Spirit; to another faith, by the same Spirit; and to another gifts of healings, by the same Spirit; and to another workings of miracles; and to another prophecy; and to another discerning of spirits; to another different kinds of languages; and to another the interpretation of languages. But the one and the same Spirit produces all of these, distributing to each one separately as he desires.

— 1 Corinthians 12:4–11

Ministry of the Holy Spirit: Resurrection to Present

The last work we are going to study is the ministry of the Holy Spirit from the resurrection of Christ to this present day. I have had the privilege to witness many great miracles, from blind eyes opening to deaf ears hearing, from cripples walking to demons fleeing. Every healing, miracle, or deliverance that you have witnessed or experienced was the work of the Holy Spirit. Every vision you saw, every prophecy you heard, every tongue that you spoke was all the work of the Holy Spirit. The Bible makes it clear that this is His specific work, doing so as He wills.

The Father laid upon Jesus our punishments and diseases (Isaiah 53:6,10), and Jesus freely chose to bear our sins, sicknesses, and curses (Isaiah 53:4,12). Because of their completed work, now healing, forgiveness, deliverance, peace, and many more blessings are available to us in the heavenly realm (Ephesians 1:3). Jesus is now seated on the throne next to the Father. Why are they seated? Because their work is done. But Who executes these promises? Who manifests these blessings in a tangible and experiential way? Beloved, that is the work of the Holy Spirit.

Now I have not covered every aspect and work of the Holy Spirit in this chapter, but I have given you a short overview of the main points. Are you beginning to see what amazing and wonderful things He does? When I meditate upon these truths, my heart overflows with joy and thankfulness. I begin to see how intimate the Holy Spirit has been in my life. From my physical birth, to the conviction of sin, to my born again experience to each healing and deliverance I have received. For most of my spiritual walk, I was unaware of how good and gracious He has been to me.

Take a moment and reflect upon these scriptures. Take some time to tell the Holy Spirit how much you appreciate Him and thank Him for all He has done for you.

Our Relationship with the Holy Spirit

We are now going to answer the third and final question: What is our personal relationship with the Holy Spirit? Because God is triune in nature, therefore our relationship with God must be three-fold. Most people view God as simply "God" and have just one type of relationship with Him. These "one type" relationships are simple, important, but not very personal. Some examples: Creator-creation, Judge-sinner and Master-servant. Since God is three unique individuals, we are going to see how our relationship differs from each member. According to that relationship, we can have deep fellowship with God.

> But as many as received him, to them he gave the right to become God's children, to those who believe in his name:
>
> — John 1:12

> "I will be to you a Father. You will be to me sons and daughters," says the Lord Almighty.
>
> — 2 Corinthians 6:18

> See how great a love the Father has given to us, that we should be called children of God!
>
> — 1 John 3:1

> ...even as He (Father) chose us in Him (Jesus)* before the foundation of the world, that we would be holy and without defect before him in love; having predestined us for adoption as children through Jesus Christ to himself, according to the good pleasure of his desire...
>
> — Ephesians 1:4–5

Note: Words in parentheses are added by the author for emphasis.

These verses show our relationship with Father God. He is not only the Father of Jesus, but He is also the Father of everyone who is alive by the Spirit through living faith. All those who believe in Jesus are His adopted children. He is Jesus's Father, but He is also our Father. We are His sons. So what is our relationship to Father God? A Father-son relationship.

Now let's see what is our relationship to Jesus:

> Let all the house of Israel therefore know certainly that God has made him both Lord and Christ, this Jesus whom you crucified.
>
> — Acts 2:36

> ...looking for the blessed hope and appearing of the glory of our great God and Savior, Jesus Christ, who gave Himself for us, that He might redeem us from all iniquity and purify for Himself a people for His own possession, zealous for good works.
>
> — Titus 2:13–14

> No longer do I call you servants, for the servant doesn't know what his lord does. But I have called you friends, for everything that I heard from my Father, I have made known to you.
>
> — John 15:15

> Let us rejoice and be exceedingly glad, and let us give the glory to Him. For the marriage of the Lamb has come, and his wife has made herself ready.
>
> — Revelation 19:7

> "It will be in that day," says Yahweh, "that you will call me 'my husband,' and no longer call me 'my master.'"
>
> — Hosea 2:16

Many people make the mistake of calling Jesus "Father." They even teach their children, saying, "Let us pray to Jesus-Papa!" Jesus is not the Father, and the Father is not Jesus. They are two different persons. Now Jesus did say that if you have seen Me, you have seen the Father (John 14:9), but that was related to nature and character, rather than the actual person. Jesus is our Lord, King, and Savior. But what did He save us for? We are saved so that we can enter into relationship with Him. Just as friends delight in each other, share their hearts, and fellowship together, in the same way Jesus desires friendship with us. But, it goes deeper than just friendship. He wants to marry us. Friendship can go only so deep, but a marriage goes even deeper in love and commitment. Jesus is our Bridegroom, Lover, and Husband, and we are His bride. So, how are we to relate to Jesus? As Lord, King, Savior, Friend, and Husband, and we are His dear friends and bride.

So then, what is our relationship to the Holy Spirit? How do we relate to Him in a personal way? Many believers don't have a clue. Let's look at Scripture and allow it to transform our world view.

> I will pray to the Father, and he will give you another Counselor, that he may be with you forever.
>
> — John 14:16

The Greek word for counselor is *parakletos,* which means "the one who walks with you, step-by-step." The Holy Spirit is described as an intimate, faithful, and committed helper. This Greek word can also be translated to mean the following: helper, advocate, strengthener, and comforter.

Jesus, after He rose from the dead, gave His disciples instructions and left. In His place He sent the Holy Spirit. Now, we are waiting for the return of Jesus. Upon His return, we will marry Him. Both Jesus and the Father are in Heaven, seated in glory, but we are on earth, in expectation of Jesus's return. So, who is with us now? It is

> *It is the person of the Holy Spirit who is given to the church... Therefore, we should make it our aim to know Him intimately.*

the Holy Spirit. We can know and have fellowship with the Father and the Son by the Spirit, but it is the Holy Spirit who is now with us. He is the guarantee that we will forever be with the Father and Jesus (2 Corinthians 1:22, 5:5 & Ephesians 1:13–14), meaning that if we already have the person of the Holy Spirit now, then we will also have the person of the Father and the Son, too.

Most believers miss this fact, and so they are not enjoying their spiritual lives to its fullness. I will marry and be with Jesus, but I now have the Holy Spirit. So marvelous is this Holy Spirit that Jesus, Himself, said it was better that He depart, for if He did not leave, He could not send His Spirit (John 16:7). Many are living in spiritual poverty, thinking they have nothing while waiting for Jesus's coming. In truth, they have the Holy Spirit, but in ignorance neglect Him. They say, "Oh, I can't wait till Jesus returns! Oh, if Jesus were here, things would be different! Oh, how blessed we would be if Jesus were here with us!" These people say such things related to their lack and inability to live a spiritually rich life now. They think it is the presence of Jesus that they need. This is in conflict with what Jesus said. Jesus said, *It is to your advantage that I leave.* So, what is the problem? The problem is that people don't know the Holy Spirit nor how to relate to Him.

I am not saying we should only desire the Holy Spirit and not Jesus. I am saying that, at this time, it is the person of the Holy Spirit who is given to the church. This is the dispensation of the Holy Spirit. Therefore, we should make it our aim to know Him intimately.

Once I understood this truth—by grace I have been given the person of the Holy Spirit—my prayer life, relationship with God, and anointing changed. I do not live in the future, but take full advantage of the present, knowing I have the Helper, faithful Holy Spirit, with me.

Let's stop a moment and evaluate our lives. Do you have a personal relationship with the Holy Spirit as helper, counselor, advocate, strengthener, and comforter? Do you lean on Him now, knowing that He is faithfully with you, every single step? Have you recognized Him? Do you cherish His presence more than the physical presence of Jesus when He walked the earth 2,000 years ago (John 16:7)? If not, then you are missing out on the greatest blessing this life can offer you. Make no mistake, He is the greatest person you can intimately know in this life!

> But the Counselor, the Holy Spirit, whom the Father will send in my name, he will teach you all things and will remind you of all that I said to you.
>
> — John 14:26

Here we see Jesus was instructing His disciples that they would have a new teacher, and this teacher would instruct them concerning all things. When Jesus walked this earth, His disciples learned directly from Him. But, Jesus did not teach or give instructions apart from the Holy Spirit (Acts 1:2). It was through the Holy Spirit that Jesus taught them, but now there would be a transition. The Holy Spirit is no longer teaching through the person of Jesus, but directly to the people of God (1 John 2:27). Did you know that it is the Holy Spirit who teaches us all things? We pray to the Father in Jesus's name for wisdom, instruction, and understanding, but the Father Himself does not instruct. Rather, He sent His Spirit (Ephesians 1:16–18), and the Holy Spirit manifests wisdom and revelation.

Whenever I have a need to know something, to understand the Word of God, or I need to be taught, I believe what Jesus said—that the Holy Spirit is with me as a teacher. I simply turn my attention to the Holy Spirit, invite His presence, and ask Him whatever I need to know. Do you have that kind of relationship with the Holy Spirit? Do you have assurance that He is with you and ready to teach you whenever you're in need? If not, turn your heart to Him and believe.

When the Counselor has come, whom I will send to you from the Father, the Spirit of truth, who proceeds from the Father, He will testify about me. You will also testify, because you have been with Me from the beginning.

— John 15:26–27

But you will receive power when the Holy Spirit has come upon you. You will be witnesses to me in Jerusalem, in all Judea and Samaria, and to the uttermost parts of the earth.

— Acts 1:8

We are His witnesses of these things; and so also is the Holy Spirit, whom God has given to those who obey Him.

— Acts 5:32

We see from Scripture that there are two types of witnesses who testify of Jesus: the Holy Spirit and us. We are called to work together to give witness of the life, death, and resurrection of Jesus. The Holy Spirit is here to do the work of testifying to the Gospel with us. He is our partner in this blessed work. We will cover this in depth in Chapter 4.

However, when He, the Spirit of truth, has come, He will guide you into all truth, for He will not speak from Himself; but whatever He hears, he will speak. He will declare to you things that are coming.

— John 16:13

Not only is the Holy Spirit our helper, teacher, and partner, but He is also our guide. The Holy Spirit is the leader and guide of God's people. He is like a faithful shepherd, leading His people into the ways of truth. He will never lead us astray.

The Holy Spirit also was Jesus's guide and leader (Matthew 4:1, Luke 4:1). If we are to walk in our identity as children of God, then we must be led by the Spirit (Romans 8:14, Galatians 5:18). The Holy Spirit will speak to us, direct us, and even tell us about the future so we can fulfill the will of God in every aspect of our lives.

Whenever I need direction in my life, or when I need to make a decision, I first look to the precious Guide that God has given me, the Holy Spirit. I turn my thoughts to Him. I call Him to come in an experiential way and guide me. Do you know He is eager to speak to you?

Let me give you a simple example. Abhilasha and I were living in Delhi, India, and one of our air conditioners broke down. It was fairly old and the technicians didn't immediately know why it was not working. So, they took it to their shop to check it out. They called and stated the cost to inspect it and the different prices to add coolant, fix the compressor, etc. They said they would buy it from us before any inspection would be done for 1,500 rupees. Abhilasha and I prayed about it, asking the Holy Spirit what we should do. I heard Him say, *Call them back and tell them you will sell it to them before inspection for 3,500 rupees.* I asked Abhilasha what she heard, and she said, *I had the impression we should sell it for 3,500 rupees.* I called them back and they were reluctant to buy it at that price. I responded, *Okay. Think about it and let us know if you change your minds.* They called back later and said they still wanted it.

The Holy Spirit knew what was wrong with the air conditioner and at what exact price to sell it. He leads us not only in the "big" decisions of life, but also in the daily, simple decisions we make.

He will glorify me, for He will take from what is mine, and will declare it to you.

— John 16:14

I have heard the statement, "If we focus too much on the Holy Spirit, we will forget to love and worship Jesus and the Father!" What does the Bible say will happen if I know the Holy Spirit deeply? He will bring me into a deeper level of worshiping and glorifying Jesus. No one knows Jesus like the Holy Spirit. No one can glorify Him better than the Holy Spirit. Jesus said that it is impossible to truly worship God without the Spirit and truth (John 4:24). Who is the Spirit of truth? The Holy Spirit. Whenever we come together to worship, or are alone in adoration, we should ask the Holy Spirit to enable us to glorify and worship Jesus and the Father. Not with words alone or according to tradition, but from deep within our spirit with the revelation of the truth.

> ...and hope doesn't disappoint us, because God's love has been poured out into our hearts through the Holy Spirit who was given to us.
>
> — Romans 5:5

> But as it is written, "Things which an eye didn't see, and an ear didn't hear, which didn't enter into the heart of man, these God has prepared for those who love Him." But to us, God revealed them through the Spirit. For the Spirit searches all things, yes, the deep things of God. For who among men knows the things of a man, except the spirit of the man, which is in him? Even so, no one knows the things of God, except God's Spirit. But we received, not the spirit of the world, but the Spirit which is from God, that we might know the things that were freely given to us by God.
>
> — 1 Corinthians 2:9–12

Except for a few specific instances, such as the the disciples' mountain experience (Matthew 17) or the Apostle Paul's Damascus road experience (Acts 9), all revelation and experience that we have of God the Father or of Jesus Christ is delivered through the person of the Holy Spirit. How did we ever experience God or His love? The Holy Spirit communicates the voice, heart, and affections of the

Father. The Holy Spirit manifests the presence of Jesus in our hearts. The Holy Spirit is the revealer of God. The Scriptures state that the Holy Spirit searches the heart of the Father, the deep things of His thoughts, emotions, and affections and reveals them to us. The Holy Spirit seeks to bring us into spiritual romance with Jesus. Not only does He communicate God's heart, but He also reveals everything that has been given to us. So much is laid up in the heavenly realm for us, such as peace, prosperity, healing, deliverance, joy, etc. (Ephesians 1:3). How can we know these things? How do we perceive them so that we can receive and walk in them? By the Spirit of God. Do you see how valuable He is? Without this important ministry of the Spirit, we are blind, deaf and unable to sense anything in the spirit realm. Without His precious grace, we are like spiritual lepers, walking around without feeling.

Or don't you know that your body is a temple of the Holy Spirit who is in you, which you have from God? You are not your own.

— 1 Corinthians 6:19

You adulterers and adulteresses, don't you know that friendship with the world is hostility toward God? Whoever therefore wants to be a friend of the world makes himself an enemy of God. Or do you think that the Scripture says in vain, "The Spirit who lives in us yearns jealously"?

— James 4:4–5

We are the temple of the Holy Spirit. He so desires and longs for intimacy with us that He chose to live inside of us. How deep can intimacy be? Marriage is deeper than friendship because of the special intimacy a husband and a wife share. Yet the Holy Spirit is in an even more intimate place than a spouse could ever be. He lives at the core of our being. Our body is a temple in which He lives, and our spirits are in union with Him and are called to minister to His indwelling presence. The Holy Spirit is a Lover, a passionate jealous

Lover that yearns for our attention, heart, and affections (Exodus 34:14).

There are times when I am in prayer that I can feel His presence manifesting inside of my body, in my chest/abdominal area. The presence becomes thick and heavy, and I can feel Him delighting in me and I in Him. The intimacy and pleasure is beyond expression. At such times, I realize that the most intimate person in my life is the Holy Spirit. Have you experienced that manifested presence on the inside of you? Have you felt His jealousy for your heart, attention and affections? Don't rush through this study, but search for the experience and revelation in each verse. Go to a quiet place, focus on the Holy Spirit, and slowly pray:

> *Holy Spirit, You are my Lover, the jealous Lover of my attention and affections. I now turn my heart and attention to You, because I want to love You. I am Your temple, and You live in me. Manifest Your presence and Your personality in a tangible way. I want to love and experience You, my Lover. Holy Spirit... I love You... Holy Spirit. You are everything to me.*

Now wait a moment in His presence.

Meditating upon these scriptures will produce a great love and appreciation for the Holy Spirit. Since we can only love after first receiving love (1 John 4:19), meditating upon who He is, what He does, and what is our relationship with Him will cause us to cherish Him. Remember, He is a lover who is after your heart, your closest companion, and He is fully with you now.

2

Intimacy with
the Holy Spirit

THE MOTIVE OF THE PURSUIT

People pursue the Holy Spirit for different reasons. One of the main reasons is to obtain the power that the Holy Spirit manifests. The Holy Spirit is the power of God, and when He manifests, incredible miracles happen. The blind see, the deaf hear, the cripples walk, demons are evicted, people see visions, weep or laugh, and many fall down under the weight of His glory. This all makes for an exciting meeting! When such power manifests on a regular basis, a minister can become quite famous and fall into a trap. Many who desire to have these manifestations in their ministry also pursue the Holy Spirit, but with wrong motives. These people seek the glory of man and not the glory of God. They want the Holy Spirit to come and be present in the meeting for their own glory and exaltation. These people perceive the Holy Spirit as a power instead of a precious person; they see Him as a means for ministry. When we do this, we devalue Him in our hearts and use Him for His power.

Early in his walk with the Lord, my good friend and fellow minister, Pastor Ankit Sajwan was seeking God for power. As he was intensely praying, the Lord spoke to him in an audible voice, saying, "Do not ask for power from Me, because I have filled fools with My power. Why won't they hear My voice? Because they have despised My affections. Won't they be like the prodigal son who asked for his inheritance and departed from Me? Without affectionate love, power corrupts and will cause your downfall. Do not say to me that you want to be My servant. For I have many servants, but few friends. Become My friend."

This is the very reason I set intimacy with the Holy Spirit as the second chapter, so that we can learn what is most important to God.

I cannot express to you how important it is to know the Holy Spirit as a person. He can be mysterious at times, in the sense of how He manifests His presence—like fire, electricity, and wind. However, in His personality, He is just like you and me, since we are created in His image. He has emotions, affections, and a tender heart. He can be made joyful or be afflicted with sorrow. Just like we enjoy spending time with our friends and family, so He enjoys us and seeks intimacy with us. But, He will never force Himself upon us. Love never seeks to control, but rather invites. So, let's open our hearts to hear His tender voice calling us to Him.

THE CHURCH'S FALSE REPRESENTATION OF THE SPIRIT

In the early years of walking with the Lord, the very few comments and references I heard about the Holy Spirit were very severe, strict, and serious. I was taught that the Father and Son are merciful, but the Holy Spirit has a temper, and you must be very reverent and on your best behavior around Him, or else you could be killed in judgment or even condemned for eternity!

This seemed extreme! Not only were these references scary, but He was called the Holy *Ghost*! Imagine a new believer thinking how he can have a relationship with a ghost! People would also say, "Now, listen carefully… He is the H-O-L-Y Spirit." What do they mean by holy? Basically, that you must be extra holy, cautious, and reverent around Him! How silly is this notion! Are the Father and Son not as holy as the Holy Spirit? They are all equally holy!

Before we dive into the Holy Spirit's true personality, I want to dismiss the two most common misconceptions about the Holy Spirit. This false representation of the Holy Spirit is personal to me. He is my dear friend and I feel provoked when people speak and teach about Him falsely.

Blasphemy of the Holy Spirit

> "Most certainly I tell you, all sins of the descendants of man will be forgiven, including their blasphemies with which they may blaspheme; but whoever may blaspheme against the Holy Spirit never has forgiveness, but is subject to eternal condemnation." —because they said, "He has an unclean spirit."
>
> — Mark 3:28–30

From the mouth of Jesus, we see that there is a severe consequence when we relate to the Holy Spirit in a specific sinful way. It is the only sin spoken of in Scripture that is unforgivable. Over the years, I have heard many different ideas and thoughts on what blasphemy of the Holy Spirit really means. The actual meaning is usually not understood, but the severity of the punishment remains in the minds of believers everywhere! Because of this one verse, many believers are actually scared of and too afraid to draw near to Him. They feel they are walking on egg shells when someone preaches or teaches about Him! Today, let me dismiss this unwarranted fear from your heart.

The word blasphemy means the act of cursing and reviling God. So, is it the act of speaking evil of the Holy Spirit? Does calling His ministry a work of the devil equate to this unforgivable sin?

The Lord has anointed me and given me a supernatural ministry. I don't believe I'm special. I believe God wants all His children to walk in the same! Everywhere I go, I teach about the Holy Spirit, preach the Gospel, and pray for the sick and demonized. Where have I heard the majority of blasphemy from? Not Hindus, not Muslims, but Christians!

The most resistant, angry, and argumentative blasphemers of the Holy Spirit are Christians who do not understand His works! I can go to many churches today and show videos of our meetings in which the deaf hear, mute speak, demons manifest and leave people, and some of the viewing Christians would say, "That is not God! That is a work of the devil!" How many "believers" do you know who call (or called) speaking in tongues a work of the devil? There are many! I was one of them!

So, are all these Christians doomed to an eternal hell because of what they said? No. If that were the case, I would also be damned and over half the church would be toast in hell!

This unforgivable sin should not be strictly understood as speaking evil of the Holy Spirit, but rather a deliberate resistance to His convicting work.

We must see the context in which Jesus spoke. In Matthew 12:22–28, Jesus was healing a blind and mute man by casting out the evil spirit that was inside of him. This demonstrative work of the Holy Spirit was done to reveal the truth about God and Jesus. Why would the sins and blasphemies committed against Jesus be forgiven, but not against the Holy Spirit? Was Jesus more merciful than the Holy Spirit? No. Jesus died for all mankind regardless of the sins committed against God. They could have done anything, but Jesus still died for them. There is no sin that His cross and blood does not cover. Regardless whether you believe it or not, Jesus died and atoned for you.

The Holy Spirit is the revealer and executor of the accomplished works of Christ.

So, what is the role and work of the Holy Spirit? He reveals and manifests the completed work of God! The Holy Spirit today does nothing of Himself, nor does He do a "new" work. He is the revealer and executor of the accomplished works of Christ. Jesus died for your sins, but who convicts you of the truth so that you can believe and receive your forgiveness? That is the Holy Spirit. If we deliberately resist His work, then we cut ourselves off from receiving God's grace.

In the context of Holy Spirit revealing Jesus as the Messiah, it was prophesied that the coming Messiah would open the eyes of the blind (Isaiah 35), and that was one of the special miracles Jesus performed (John 9:31–33). The Holy Spirit was saying to everyone, "Look! Jesus is the Messiah! I am proving it now! Believe and receive your salvation!" But what did the Pharisees do? They called Him a devil, and by doing so, they cut themselves off from the convicting work of the Holy Spirit. The Holy Spirit did not cut them off, but rather they cut themselves off from Him!

Friend, the Holy Spirit enjoys and delights to lavish upon you every good and precious gift from the Father. He will not force it upon you, but He opens up your eyes to see it and enables you to receive it. That is called faith. But if we say "No" to His work, we will never be able to believe and receive God's grace, including eternal life.

Ananias and Sapphira

The other most feared verse of scripture concerning the Holy Spirit is the death of Ananias and Sapphira, and it happened in church! I think it is so comical how pastors preach that the Holy Spirit slayed them dead in judgment! How far it is from the truth! This is mostly taught by pastors and believers who are law-based in their reasoning, and who don't understand the Gospel of grace.

As we read Acts 5, it appears that Peter supernaturally knows they did not bring all the money they got from selling their land. Peter then speaks a word of judgment against them, and they immediately die. Because Peter supernaturally knew and because they died immediately, many come to the conclusion that God killed them.

First of all, I want to say that this interpretation is not consistent with the New Testament teachings on the nature and character of Christ. People who do not understand the difference between the old and new covenant often make this mistake.

When Jesus came, a new era came with Him. That Person and that era is called grace. The Gospel is called the Gospel of the Grace of God (Acts 20:24). Jesus is full of grace (John 1:14), and from Jesus, we receive only one thing—grace (John 1:16). Did Jesus ever slay anyone in judgment? Did Jesus ever put disease, a curse, affliction, calamity or death upon anyone? No. Nor does the Father. For Jesus only did what He saw the Father do (John 5:19–20, 6:38, 14:10). God has reconciled the world to Himself and is no longer counting or holding men's sins against them (2 Corinthians 5:18–20), and He has given us a message of reconciliation. Not a message of judgment and death! God is not in the business of judging and destroying people, but rather saving them (Luke 9:51–56).

If Jesus and the Father are saving mankind and no longer holding their sins against them, but the Holy Spirit is holding their sins against them, judging them and destroying them, then we have a big problem with our theology! We have a divided Godhead! There is no more unity! The Holy Spirit came only to manifest the accomplished works of the cross. Judgment and death were not part of those works. Jesus bore all judgment and death upon Himself for us! The Holy Spirit came to manifest the blessings of God upon mankind. Last time I checked, judgment and death were not gifts of the Spirit!

Why did Jesus pour out the Holy Spirit upon His church? So they would represent Jesus to a lost and broken world. The Spirit comes to represent Jesus through the believer! He empowers us to display the same nature and ministry through our lives.

You must be thinking… "Well, then why did they die?!" Let's look at one more scripture before I answer that question.

> Jesus therefore said to them again, "Peace be to you. As the Father has sent me, even so I send you." When he had said this, he breathed on them, and said to them, "Receive the Holy Spirit! If you forgive anyone's sins, they have been forgiven them. If you retain anyone's sins, they have been retained."
>
> — John 20:21–23

This is the first time that Jesus gives the Holy Spirit to His disciples. Why was He given? So that we would partner with Him, preaching and demonstrating the Gospel to all nations (John 15:26–27, Acts 5:30–32, Luke 24:49). Immediately after giving them the Spirit, Jesus says something very strange: *If you forgive anyone's sins, they have been forgiven them. If you retain anyone's sins, they have been retained.*

Is that strange? What was Jesus intending to say? He was saying this: I'm leaving now, and you, through partnership with the Holy Spirit, must be My representatives. I am giving you incredible authority and responsibility. Even to the degree that eternal matters lay in your hands. Now represent Me as I properly represented My Father.

Beloved, we fail to see how much authority we truly have! If you are dying of cancer and, medically speaking, are hopeless, and you go to a church that does not preach Jesus as a healer… guess what is going to happen? You are going to die! If you go to a church and the preacher does not preach Jesus as the Savior of our sins… what is going to happen? People are not going to know the truth, and they will consequently go to hell. It has nothing to do with God, but everything to do with us!

Why did Ananias and Sapphira die? Because Peter cursed them with words of judgment and death! Was there any mercy or compassion in Peter's words? No. Was there any opportunity for repentance? No. Did he forgive their sins or retain them? Peter did not represent Jesus in this scenario, and his words had an effect. Listen to what he said to Sapphira, "Behold, the feet of those who have buried your husband are at the door, and they will carry you out." This was not the only instance when Peter was unmerciful and full of judgment (see Acts 8:18–23). Sometimes, we think that everything the apostles said and did was of God, and we fail to recognize that they were people, just like us, growing in their walk with God.

The Holy Spirit did not slay Ananias and Sapphira. If He slayed them for lying and giving only a portion of what they owned, then why is He not slaying pastors, leaders, and believers all across this world right now who are deliberately stealing, committing adultery, hating, having abortions, and gossiping?

Do not be afraid of the Holy Spirit. Do honor, love, and revere Him—not out of fear of judgment, but rather out of the truth of His love and kindness toward you (Romans 2:4, 1 John 4:19).

UNDERSTANDING THE HOLY SPIRIT'S PERSONALITY

To understand and know the Holy Spirit's personality better, we are going to look at a few scriptures.

> How much worse punishment do you think he will be judged worthy of who has trodden under foot the Son of God, and has counted the blood of the covenant with which he was sanctified an unholy thing, and has insulted the Spirit of grace?
>
> — Hebrews 10:29

> For the law of the Spirit of life in Christ Jesus made me free from the law of sin and of death.
>
> — Romans 8:2

Though the context of the first verse is a warning against apostasy, the Scripture tells us a very important aspect of the Holy Spirit; He is the Spirit of grace. What is grace? Grace is unmerited love, goodness, and kindness expressed to someone who is not worthy to receive it. The Holy Spirit is loving, good, and kind to people who are not worthy of His goodness. Though we should have a heart to honor, respect, and revere Him, we need to realize that He is gracious and the Spirit of grace. Nowhere is it written that He is the Spirit of wrath and anger. From His presence and personality flow unmerited love and kindness. He is just like Jesus in His great compassion for us. Knowing that He is the Spirit of grace, I am confident to approach Him, just as we are encouraged to approach Jesus' throne of grace with boldness (Hebrews 4:16). Though I am not perfect in everything I do, I know I can be intimate with Him and expect to receive His love, affection, and presence because He is gracious. He delights in expressing that grace to us.

He is also the Spirit of life. What is life? Peace is life. Joy is life. Love is life. Healing, deliverance, forgiveness, and freedom are life. Hearing His voice and spending time in His presence causes our spirits to receive life, to enjoy pleasure (Psalm 36:8). If you will develop a deep intimacy with the Holy Spirit, there will be an evidence of life in your being—such deep joy and peace others can immediately recognize.

> John testified, saying, "I have seen the Spirit descending like a dove out of heaven, and it remained on him. I didn't recognize him, but he who sent me to baptize in water, he said to me, 'On whomever you will see the Spirit descending, and remaining on him, the same is He who baptizes in the Holy Spirit.'"
>
> — John 1:32–33

Out of all the animals in creation to choose, the Holy Spirit came in the form of a dove. Have you ever thought why? The devil chose a snake, because a snake best fits his personality: stealthy, impersonal, independent, and a predator that seeks to devour. But what characteristics does a dove have that best describe the Holy Spirit?

A dove is pure white, which represents holiness and purity. The dove is the world symbol for peace. Another amazing aspect of doves is that they only have one mate and live faithfully with that one. This reveals the Holy Spirit's gracious faithfulness to us.

There are other Scripture references where the Holy Spirit manifested in a whirlwind, fire, and incredible power that caused an earthquake (Acts 2:1–4, 4:31, 16:25–26). But, this is related to His works, rather than His nature. In His nature, the Holy Spirit is very peaceful, gracious, and kind, holy, pure, and faithful.

What was the Holy Spirit's motive for descending upon Jesus? John 1:32 states that He came, descending upon Jesus, to remain. The Holy Spirit is a Lover who is looking for a lover. He is looking for a place to abide, where He can have friendship, intimacy, and love. The Holy Spirit found that place in Jesus. Jesus loved the Holy Spirit and was sensitive to His presence wherever He went. We will discuss this in greater detail in Chapter 3.

Jesus is our model, and if the Holy Spirit remained upon Jesus, then He wants to remain on us. The question in our hearts should not be, "Will the Holy Spirit descend and remain on me?" Rather, our question should be, "Will *I* affectionately host His presence and treat Him with the love and respect He deserves?"

The Greatest Commandment

Now we are going to look at two critical commandments that are related to the Holy Spirit.

> One of the scribes came, and heard them questioning together. Knowing that He had answered them well, they asked Him, "Which commandment is the greatest of all?" Jesus answered, "The greatest is, 'Hear, Israel, the Lord our God, the Lord is one: you shall love the Lord your God with all your heart, and with all your soul, and with all your mind, and with all your strength.' This is the first commandment."
>
> — Mark 12:28–30

According to the law God gave through Moses, the greatest commandment is directly related to our loving relationship with the Lord. We are called to love God. But, which member of the Godhead are we to love? Jesus did not say, "Love the Father with all your heart." Jesus said that we are to love God. Just as we learned in Chapter 1 that God is triune, so then our love must be for each one of them equally. We are not to love only Jesus and neglect the Holy Spirit, nor are we to focus only on the Father. We are to love, cherish, and have a deep relationship with each of them.

Most believers don't relate to God as a triune being. Instead, they just have a vague relationship with only "God." But, according to this commandment, we are to love them equally. After I came to know the Holy Spirit as a tender, affectionate person, I realized this commandment was directly related to Him. I am called to love the Holy Spirit just as much as I am called to love Jesus! Neglecting to love the Holy Spirit would be to neglect this great commandment. That is like saying to me, "Oh, I really like to fellowship with you, but I don't value your wife, nor do I ever want to see her or talk to her!" If someone said that to me, I would question if he is really my friend! Beloved, let us seek to love this precious Holy Spirit as we would Jesus or the Father.

Now Jesus did not just say, "The greatest commandment is to love God." Rather, He said, "The greatest commandment is to love God with all your heart, all your soul, all your mind, and all your strength." Honestly thinking, that is very detailed! In saying this, Jesus did not leave any part or portion of our being out! Not just with our heart, but with all of our being!

Let us look into the Greek to see exactly what Jesus is talking about:

ENGLISH	GREEK	MEANING
Heart	*Kardia*	The center of our lives, the center of our personality, love, and desire
Soul	*Suche*	Our affections, free-will, desires, passions, and emotions
Mind	*Deanoina*	Our thoughts, understanding, attention, and meditation
Strength	*Ischus*	Our physical strength, skills, abilities, physical and financial possessions and wealth

Do you see how much God wants us to love Him? Nothing is exempt from this list, because God desires all of us. It is not through religious strength of obeying the Law that will make us true lovers of God, but rather receiving His great love for us and allowing that love to enable us to love Him back. Remember we are no longer under the Law but under grace, and grace is more powerful than the Law! The Holy Spirit is a jealous Lover (James 4:4–5), and He yearns for our love, affection, and attention. This is what He desires most from our lives, and also what He freely gives us.

Regardless if you are a full-time minister or a housewife raising a bunch of kids, single or married, the invitation to a deep, intimate walk of love with God is for everyone. Don't allow religious perspectives to discourage this adventure of love! Jump into the deep end!

> God is spirit; those who worship Him must worship in spirit and truth.
>
> — John 4:24

> He said with a loud voice, "Fear the Lord, and give Him glory; for the hour of His judgment has come. Worship Him who made the heavens, the earth, the sea, and the springs of waters!"
>
> — Revelation 14:7

> I fell down before his feet to worship him. He said to me, "Look! Don't do it! I am a fellow bondservant with you and with your brothers who hold the testimony of Jesus. Worship God, for the testimony of Jesus is the Spirit of Prophecy."
>
> — Revelation 19:10

> He said to me, "See you don't do it! I am a fellow bondservant with you and with your brothers, the prophets, and with those who keep the words of this book. Worship God."
>
> — Revelation 22:9

In the Bible, every command to worship is directed toward God. There is no Scripture in the Bible that says we are to worship only the Father, nor to worship only Jesus. We are to worship God. Remember that God is triune, and we are to worship each of them.

According to the Scriptures we just read, in relation to the Holy Spirit, we are directed to (1) worship, (2) fear, and (3) give glory to Him, just as we are called to worship, fear, and give glory to the Father and Jesus.

What is worship? It is a response from our spirit to the grace and truth of God. When we see how wonderful Jesus is, how humble, loving, and caring He is, we worship Him. When we see how great and majestic our Father is and how sacrificial He was in giving us His Son, we respond with worship. In the same way, we can respond to the Holy Spirit. In Chapter 1, we covered the amazing works that the Holy Spirit did and does. In response to those truths, we can worship Him.

FELLOWSHIP WITH THE SPIRIT

Let's now look into practical ways we can have fellowship with the Holy Spirit.

> The grace of the Lord Jesus Christ, the love of God, and the fellowship of the Holy Spirit, be with you all. Amen.
>
> — 2 Corinthians 13:14

This verse states that the communion of the Holy Spirit can be with us. This word "communion" in the Greek is *koinonia*, which means: fellowship, partnership, camaraderie, communion, conversation, and the exchanging of thoughts and emotions.

Just as marriage requires time to develop deep intimacy, we need to spend time in our relationship with the Holy Spirit. If I do not talk to my wife for five days because my priorities are wrong, then I am distancing myself from her. Just as marriage requires intentional, quality time to be spent with each other, we need to make loving and knowing the Holy Spirit a priority. Deep fellowship with the Holy Spirit will not happen by accident. It should be intentional, but not based upon our works or striving.

I will give you an example. Many years ago, I was in Miraz, Maharashtra. I was conducting a training seminar for pastors, leaders, and lay-leaders in that area. During the evenings, we held a three-day healing meeting. It was a wonderful time, and God did many miracles, such as the blind seeing, deaf hearing, and many sick were healed. On the third evening, the last day of the event, after the meeting began, one of the young men who attended the training approached me and asked, "How many days do you fast before such meetings? How many hours do you pray?" This young man was looking for a formula. Beloved, relationship is not based upon a formula, like if I spent so many hours with my wife, I would know her. I will truly know her when she opens her heart up to me, and from heart-to-heart fellowship, our love and relationship is deepened.

What does fellowship require? It requires time, intentionality, desire, openness of heart, and love. I smiled and answered the young man, "Actually, I have not fasted in years, and I don't do much intercessory prayer. I just spend time with the Holy Spirit, who is my Friend and my Lover." He gave a puzzled look and walked off. Beloved, if we focus on loving and knowing Him, His presence and power will automatically be with us. Jesus taught that our motive for fasting should come from a longing to be with Him, not to obtain something from Him (Matthew 9:15).

So, how do we practically fellowship with Him? I will give you several examples from my personal life.

First, I spend time alone with the Holy Spirit, in a quiet place where I will not be distracted. Then, I focus my attention upon Him, and I invite Him to come and be with me. Now when we invite the Holy

Spirit to come, we need to understand that He is already inside of us and with us (John 14:17). I am not inviting Him in unbelief, thinking that He is far away from me, but rather calling Him to intimacy with me. For example, I might be in one room of my house and my wife in another room. She is with me in the house, but we are not focused on each other. I call her to come and be close to me. In the same way, the Holy Spirit lives inside of our body, as does our own spirit. This invitation is a call to fellowship, communion, and intimacy.

This invitation is a call to fellowship, communion, and intimacy.

Once I have invited Him, I will seek to experience His presence. Just as my wife comes near me and I hug her and hold her near, we can embrace the presence of the Holy Spirit and hold Him near. As I am holding my wife, my attention and affection is upon her. In the same way, we can embrace His presence and place our attention and affections upon Him. Once we are in that place, I will speak words of love to the Holy Spirit. My focus is not prayer, nor the words that I am speaking. My focus is on Him and His presence. I will speak words of love every few minutes. I say things like, "Holy Spirit, You are so precious to me. I love You, Holy Spirit. You are beautiful and wonderful. I enjoy being with You. You mean everything to me. I am Your temple, and You abide in me. You are my Lover, and I give You my affections."

When I say these things, I speak them slowly to Him. Often, His presence will increase. Sometimes, His presence is so strong that I don't want to speak, because I am overcome by Him. I may do this for 5–10 minutes. At other times, it lasts more than an hour. I do not put a time limit or a time-based goal on my fellowship with Him. I do it because I love Him and because He loves me and wants to be with me. Since the Holy Spirit is in us and with us, we can do this anywhere, at anytime.

If you are not familiar with sensing and experiencing His presence, then this might sound very foreign to you, but do not be discouraged. As you intentionally practice this, you will begin to experience Him. The experience is not the goal, but fellowshipping with Him is. Whether His presence is heavy or so light I can barely feel it, that does not matter. What does matter is that He loves me and I choose to love Him back. The most enjoyable and pleasurable times in my life have been with the Holy Spirit in this manner. Beloved, He is eagerly waiting for you!

At such times of intimacy, I often see visions and the Holy Spirit speaks to me. Other times, the joy of the Holy Spirit comes upon me and I start laughing. Sometimes, I laugh so hard I can barely breath. My mind does not understand why I am laughing, because there is nothing funny to perceive. But, my spirit can see His smile, sense His joy, and at times I feel Him tickling me. The Holy Spirit loves to have fun with us.

Second, I will go somewhere alone and talk with the Holy Spirit, just as I would talk with a friend. I often go to parks, in the woods, or walk around somewhere quiet. While I am walking, I just talk to Him. I am not interceding for others, nor am I praying through a list of needs. What do two friends talk about when they get together? If you've ever had a good friend, then you know you can spend hours talking about various things. Those things may be work, family life, hobbies, projects, personal goals, etc. When we talk as friends, we share what we think, what we feel, and what we desire. Then, we listen to our friend's response. This dialogue is two-sided: hearing and speaking. In the same way, I talk to the Holy Spirit. I tell Him how I am feeling, how work is going, how my family life is, and my goals in life. I do this for ten minutes to an hour. What is my goal? My goal is friendship and fellowship with my God, the Holy Spirit.

In various meetings, I will often stand up and give words of knowledge and prophecies over people, and many miracles happen, such as instantaneous healing, deliverances, and spiritual encounters. Many people come up to me and ask me how I hear the Holy Spirit's voice and how they can learn to do the same. They are looking for a formula, a special key to perceive the presence and voice of the Holy Spirit. I tell people that I spend time talking with the Holy

Spirit, just as I would a friend.

See, whether I am walking in a park chatting with the Holy Spirit about what foods I like to eat or in a healing meeting praying for the sick, the situation does not change for me. I seek fellowship with the Holy Spirit. Someone would suggest that talking to the Holy Spirit in a park about non-ministry issues is not being very spiritual. I disagree. How did I learn to hear the Holy Spirit's voice? While talking to Him in the woods, where no one was watching or listening (Matthew 6:6). After a while, I would hear Him respond to me. After months and years of such fellowship, my spirit has become accustomed to His voice.

So, when I am in a meeting in front of thousands and the Holy Spirit says to me, "There is a woman here who has been blind in her left eye for three years," I can hear and recognize Him. The voice in the park is the same voice in front of thousands. If we don't value His presence and His voice in the secret place, then we should not expect to hear His voice in the meeting (Matthew 6:6).

Spend time each day, or every other day, talking to the Holy Spirit. Even if it is just 5–10 minutes, start this new habit of fellowshipping with Him. He loves to hear your voice and is waiting to respond to you.

Third, I will worship the Holy Spirit, just as I worship the Father and the Son. Whether alone or in a group, I spend some time including the precious Holy Spirit in my times of worship.

Fourth, I invite the Holy Spirit into life situations. When I wake up in the morning, I make it a point to think of the Father, Jesus and the Holy Spirit. I will often say, "Good Morning, precious Holy Spirit!" During the day as I minister, I will invite Him into my daily work. If I lost something, I will invite Him and ask Him to help me. If I have any marriage or family decision or issue to attend to, I talk to Him and ask Him for His thoughts. Before I make a decision to travel anywhere for ministry, or buy a car, or purchase land, whether big or small, I always invite Him and ask Him to guide me. Even when I am exhausted and tired, the Holy Spirit wants to be with me.

One day when I was extremely exhausted from traveling for over a week non-stop, the Holy Spirit said to me, "I want to be your pillow," and smiled at me. Isn't that sweet? He is so caring and loving!

THE MOST PRECIOUS GIFT OF ALL

We are now going to look at the various gifts God has given to us. We can see that the Father has already given us every spiritual blessing, and those blessings are in the heavens, waiting for us to receive it by faith (Ephesians 1:3). There is physical healing available, as well as deliverance and freedom from all bondages. Peace, joy, prosperity, favor, forgiveness, eternal life, etc., are all there, and they are ours. But, do you know what is the greatest gift of all? Let us look at a few scriptures before we answer this important question.

> Peter said to them, "Repent, and be baptized, every one of you, in the name of Jesus Christ for the forgiveness of sins, and you will receive the gift of the Holy Spirit."
>
> — Acts 2:38

> ...saying, "Give me also this power, that whomever I lay my hands on may receive the Holy Spirit." But Peter said to him, "May your silver perish with you, because you thought you could obtain the gift of God with money! You have neither part nor lot in this matter, for your heart isn't right before God. Repent therefore of this, your wickedness, and ask God if perhaps the thought of your heart may be forgiven you.
>
> — Acts 8:19–22

> They of the circumcision who believed were amazed, as many as came with Peter, because the gift of the Holy Spirit was also poured out on the Gentiles.
>
> — Acts 10:45

Everything that we receive from God is a gift by His grace. But, there is a special gift above all gifts. You see, God gave us forgiveness, eternal life, and joy. These are all gifts, but the special gift is the Giver Himself. The Giver is greater than the gifts He gives. God gave Himself to us as a gift. The Father and the Son gave us the most precious gift of all, the gift of the Holy Spirit. We get many blessings by His grace, but the greatest of them is the Blesser.

Do you see that the person of the Holy Spirit is the greatest gift of God? You can delight in the joy of the Lord. But, it is even better to delight in the Lord of all joy—the Holy Spirit! We receive the gift of eternal life, but we also receive the Spirit of life (Romans 8:2). The Holy Spirit is the first-fruits of our relationship with God. While on this earth, we get Him fully. We are one with Christ now by the Spirit, but we will be united with Christ, face-to-face, at His coming. We, as the bride, yearn for Jesus to return because we don't have Him fully now (Revelation 22:17), and we are longing for that city where our beloved Father dwells (Hebrews 11:13–16). But, we have the person of the Holy Spirit now. This gives us full assurance that, if we have the Holy Spirit now, we will soon be united with our beloved Jesus and Father (Ephesians 1:13–14). Knowing that the Spirit is fully with me now inspires me to know Him and to cherish that person of the Godhead that the Father and Son has entrusted to me now.

NOT POWER BUT A PERSONALITY

Some understand and teach that the Holy Spirit is only the power of God and view Him as a mysterious being or an impersonal force that fulfills the will of God. This is a lie, and in concluding this chapter we are going to look at a few scriptures related to His personality, so that we can correctly understand Him.

But the one and the same Spirit produces all of these, distributing to each one separately as he desires.

— 1 Corinthians 12:11

Don't quench the Spirit.

— 1 Thessalonians 5:19

The Holy Spirit has His own free-will, and in regard to manifesting the gifts, He does so as He wills. In other aspects, the Holy Spirit speaks and ministers to people as the Father and Jesus will (John 16:13), but related to the gifts, the Holy Spirit has free reign to exercise the fullness of His desires. The Holy Spirit is a passionate being, described as a consuming fire of love. He does not seek to control, but rather invites us into partnership and relationship. We can quench His passionate desires by resisting Him, just as we can quench a fire with water.

For it seemed good to the Holy Spirit, and to us, to lay no greater burden on you than these necessary things:

— Acts 15:28

As the apostles were seeking the Lord's guidance in discipling the new Gentile believers, the Holy Spirit manifested His will to them by revealing to them His pleasure in their decision making. The Holy Spirit smiled and gave them the "okay" to go ahead, thus revealing that He has His own mind and thoughts.

Don't grieve the Holy Spirit of God, in whom you were sealed for the day of redemption.

— Ephesians 4:30

According to the Greek, a better translation for the word grieve is vex or torment. Did you know we can torment the Holy Spirit? Not only does He have His own mind, thoughts, and will, but He also has emotions. We can afflict and torment Him when we turn away from His loving guidance and rebel against Him. Just as a dove is sensitive and easily frightened, even so the emotions of the Holy Spirit are very sensitive.

> Now I beg you, brothers, by our Lord Jesus Christ, and by the love of the Spirit, that you strive together with me in your prayers to God for me.
>
> — Romans 15:30

Not only does the Holy Spirit manifest the love of Jesus and the Father to us (Romans 5:5), but He has His own love, as well. If the Holy Spirit only conveyed the love of others, then He would not be a complete person. But, this Scripture proves that He has His own love and affections, thus completing our view of Him as a total being.

Have you experienced His personal love for you? This is an invitation to know Him personally and develop a deep relationship with Him.

3

The Model of Jesus

Subconscious Beliefs

The beginning years of my ministry were very exciting. I was working with several pastors in a large church, serving them in various ways, from administration and helps to teaching and discipleship. I learned many things from them, and I cherish those years. During that time, I developed a mindset that most believers have. Due to my experiences and what others said to me, without knowing it, I subconsciously accepted a belief system about the life of Jesus.

All of us believe that God is all powerful and that Jesus did incredible miracles on earth. God can do anything. But, the problem we faced was that He was doing very little among us, speaking comparatively to what we read about in the Gospels and the Book of Acts, concerning the miraculous power of God. Every week, I would go with my pastors to make hospital calls. If any member of our church was in the hospital, we surely went to express our love and care for them.

During those hospital visits, year after year, I noticed something strange. We prayed for so many, but none of them were instantly healed before our eyes. All those on death's bed were buried. Puzzled by the experience, I asked my pastors one day why they were not healed. The moment they looked into my eyes, I could perceive the same puzzling feeling inside of them. They replied something like this: "I don't know. I don't understand why they are not healed either. We just keep on doing what we are doing and try to believe and love people."

To love people is the foundation of the ministry, and without love, power means nothing (1 Corinthians 13:2). But, without power, love cannot be fully expressed. We should not continue to walk in ignorance but know what the will of the Lord is (Ephesians 5:17). Is there a reason why so many people are not healed? Is there a reason for the lack of miracles? Why don't we see the Gospels and the Book of Acts alive in our ministries and churches today? From what I know, there are many reasons for the lack of miracles. But, I want to focus on one of the main reasons in this chapter.

Many people view the life of Jesus incorrectly, and I was one of them. From one bumper stickers that read, "Next time you think you're perfect, try walking on water," to remarks like, "Don't look to me! I'm not Jesus!" Or another example: "Oh, if only Jesus were here, that person would be healed." From pulpit preaching to daily comments, most of us have believed this lie: Jesus was able to do all the miracles He did, heal all the sick, and cast out every demon because He was the Son of God. We can't do such things because we are nothing, but He is everything.

Those who believe this often make statements such as, "If the sick were healed in Jesus' day, it was because the Son of God was on earth at that time. Of course all the demons were driven out! They could not stand against the Son of God! Raising the dead? Who could do that other than Jesus, the Son of God? Of course Jesus can do anything! He is the Son of God!"

This kind of thinking exalts Jesus to a special place of life and ministry that we could never achieve. If we dare to try, then "believers" would mock us and say, "Who do you think you are? Jesus!?" If the same miracles and healings do not happen in our lives as they did with Jesus, we then have a theological excuse: "I cannot because I am not Jesus, the Son of God."

THE TRUTH

I have come to believe something that has radically transformed the way I think. This new belief is a pillar of faith in my spirit. It also exalts Jesus higher and gives Him even greater glory than the previous statement I made. What is it? Jesus did everything on earth as a man without using any of His privileges as the Son of God. I am dedicating the rest of this chapter to explaining in detail how this was possible. But why is this so important? First, let's compare the two statements.

Traditional Belief: Jesus was able to do all the miracles recorded in the Gospels because He was the Son of God.

Truth: Jesus accomplished all the miracles not by operating as the Son of God, but as a man fully submitted to the Father and empowered by the Holy Spirit.

The traditional belief gives us an excuse if the miracles are not happening, a reason to disbelieve. The truth, however, inspires us to a place of faith where the miraculous is possible. I believe that if Jesus was able to accomplish them as a man, then I should be motivated to do the same.

Let us look at a foundational scripture for this teaching.

Jesus accomplished all the miracles not by operating as the Son of God, but as a man fully submitted to the Father and empowered by the Holy Spirit.

Have this in your mind, which was also in Christ Jesus, who, existing in the form of God, didn't consider equality with God a thing to be grasped, but emptied himself, taking the form of a servant, being made in the likeness of men. And being found in human form, he humbled himself, becoming obedient to death, yes, the death of the cross. Therefore, God also highly exalted Him and gave to Him the name which is above every name; that at the name of Jesus every knee should bow, of those in heaven, those on earth, and those under the earth, and that every tongue should confess that Jesus Christ is Lord, to the glory of God the Father."

— Philippians 2:5–11

Let's focus on verses 6 and 7. These scriptures state that Jesus, as the Son of God, was equal with God. All the members of the Godhead are equal in knowledge, power, and capacity. Jesus was just as much God as the Father or the Holy Spirit. But, He did something amazing. He *emptied Himself.* In the Greek, this means that Jesus made Himself nothing. How did He become empty? What part of Him was made nothing? Jesus, while coming to be born on this earth, laid aside all of His omniscience, power, and capacity as God and, in fully becoming a man, limited Himself. He was still God in the flesh, but He did not use any of His privileges or powers as God.

It is clear from Scripture that Jesus did not know everything while He walked on this earth. Consider these verses:

When Jesus heard it, he marveled and said to those who followed, "Most certainly I tell you, I haven't found so great a faith, not even in Israel."

— Matthew 8:10

Seeing a fig tree afar off having leaves, he came to see if perhaps he might find anything on it. When he came to it, he found nothing but leaves, for it was not the season for figs.

— Mark 11:13

Immediately, Jesus, perceiving in Himself that the power had gone out from Him, turned around in the crowd and asked, "Who touched my clothes?" His disciples said to Him, "You see the multitude pressing against You, and You say, 'Who touched me?'" He looked around to see her who had done this thing.

— Mark 5:30–32

All of these Scriptures reveal that Jesus laid aside His omniscience and limited Himself to know as a man knows. How can someone who knows everything marvel? Why did Jesus look for figs on the tree if He knew beforehand that there were none? Why was Jesus asking about and looking for someone who touched Him if He already knew who she was? What supernatural things Jesus knew on this earth, He knew them by the Holy Spirit.

Even after looking at these Scriptures, still others may disagree, saying, "Jesus could do whatever He wanted because He was the Son of God." If this statement is true, then Jesus threw away a wonderful opportunity to prove it at His home town.

He could do no mighty work there, except that he laid His hands on a few sick people and healed them. He marveled because of their unbelief.

— Mark 6:5–6

This Scripture clearly shows that Jesus could not do any mighty miracles there. It does not say, "would not," but "could not." What better place to perform miracles to prove that He was the Son of God than at His unbelieving hometown?

See, Jesus's life was a model for us. If He operated as the Son of God, then we could never do the things that He did, because we are not God. But, if He knew things by the Spirit and operated as a man, then we are inspired to be like Him.

Let us look at the first miracle Jesus performed. After Jesus turned the water into wine, this is written about Him.

> This beginning of His signs Jesus did in Cana of Galilee and revealed His glory; and His disciples believed in Him."
>
> — John 2:11

Why didn't Jesus perform miracles prior to this event? Is there a reason why this was the first miracle? Was there something necessary for His miracle ministry? Let's look at a few more Scriptures.

> Now when all the people were baptized, Jesus also had been baptized, and was praying. The sky was opened, and the Holy Spirit descended in a bodily form like a dove on Him; and a voice came out of the sky, saying "You are my beloved Son. In you I am well pleased."
>
> — Luke 3:21–22

> Jesus returned in the power of the Spirit into Galilee, and news about Him spread through all the surrounding area.
>
> — Luke 4:14

> The Spirit of the Lord is on me, because He has anointed me to preach good news to the poor. He has sent me to heal the brokenhearted, to proclaim release to the captives, recovering of sight to the blind, to deliver those who are crushed..."
>
> — Luke 4:18

> ...even Jesus of Nazareth, how God anointed Him with the Holy Spirit and with power, who went about doing good and healing all who were oppressed by the devil, for God was with Him.
>
> — Acts 10:38

These Scriptures reveal that prior to the descending of the Holy Spirit upon Jesus, He did not heal one sick person, cast out any demons, raise any dead, or perform any miracles. It was only after the Holy Spirit manifested Himself on Jesus that such miracles happened.

Only after being filled with the Holy Spirit, wherever Jesus went, demons started freaking out and revealing themselves (Mark 1:21–28, 34). Have you ever noticed that demons, prior to the descending of the Holy Spirit, never manifested in the synagogues when Jesus was there? We have no record of demons ever manifesting, screaming, or being fearful of Jesus prior to the Holy Spirit descending upon Him. Why? Because He so stripped Himself of His Godlikeness and so became man that even demons could not recognize Him. Satan tempted Jesus only after He was filled with the Spirit of God. Not even Satan could recognize Him! But, when the Holy Spirit descended, Jesus and the Holy Spirit became one. The Christ means "the anointed one." To anoint, in the Greek, means "to smear." God anointed Jesus with the Holy Spirit, meaning the Father smeared and covered Jesus with the presence, power, and person of the Holy Spirit. The demons were reacting to the presence and power of the Holy Spirit, who was on Jesus. Jesus performed every miracle as a man submitted to Father God through the person of the Holy Spirit.

Now, let's look at how Jesus was guided to perform the miracles:

> Jesus therefore answered them, "Most certainly, I tell you, the Son can do nothing of Himself, but what He sees the Father doing. For whatever things He does, these the Son also does likewise. For the Father has affection for the Son and shows him all things that He Himself does. He will show Him greater works than these, that you may marvel.
>
> — John 5:19–20

"For I have come down from heaven, not to do My own will, but the will of Him who sent Me."

— John 6:38

These Scriptures show that Jesus performed each and every miracle by the Father's guidance and command. Jesus so emptied Himself that He was unable to do such miracles by Himself. He was completely dependent upon the Father. How did the Father reveal His will and guide Jesus? This is where the Holy Spirit's role comes in. The Father reveals His will to the Holy Spirit, and then the Holy Spirit reveals that to us. The Holy Spirit is the communicator and revealer of the Father's will (Luke 4:1, Matthew 10:19–20).

Sometimes we think that the life of Jesus was incredibly different and unique compared to our own experiences with God. Some believe that Jesus automatically and always knew the Father's will, but this is not true. Jesus came to know the will of the Father through the Holy Spirit just as we can know it today. The Holy Spirit is the channel of communication from God to us and the power that fulfills the revealed will of God. It came to Jesus by impressions, visions, dreams, or angels. These are the revelation gifts of the Holy Spirit that are given to the church (1 Corinthians 12:7–10). We will learn about these in greater detail in Chapter 6.

Jesus and the Holy Spirit had a very intimate relationship. Jesus's focus, attention, and affections were always on the Holy Spirit, even when people were demanding of Jesus's time and energy. Let's read a short story about a woman who was healed. As we read this story, do not focus on the healing aspect, but rather on the relationship Jesus had with the Holy Spirit.

When Jesus returned, the multitude welcomed Him, for they were all waiting for Him. Behold, there came a man named Jairus, and he was a ruler of the synagogue. He fell down at Jesus's feet and begged Him to come into his house, for he had an only daughter, about twelve years of age, and she was dying. But as he went, the multitudes pressed against him. A woman who had a flow of blood for twelve years, who had spent all her living on physicians and could not be healed by any, came behind Him, and touched the fringe of His cloak, and immediately the flow of her blood stopped. Jesus said, "Who touched me?" When all denied it, Peter and those with Him said, "Master, the multitudes press and jostle you, and you say, 'Who touched me?'" But Jesus said, "Someone did touch me, for I perceived that power has gone out of me." When the woman saw that she was not hidden, she came trembling and, falling down before Him, declared to Him in the presence of all the people the reason why she had touched Him and how she was healed immediately. He said to her, "Daughter, cheer up. Your faith has made you well. Go in peace."

— Luke 8:40-48

Picture yourself as Jesus. You just came back and are welcomed by so many people. How many were there? We don't have an exact idea. It could have been hundreds or, more likely, thousands. Imagine that hundreds of people are calling out your name. Others are pushing each other just to get a glimpse of you. Surely there are many people calling out and inviting you to their homes for dinner and some inviting you to pray for their sick at home. Others are grabbing at you, touching you, because they heard wonderful stories of the sick being healed and the tormented being delivered. It was complete madness!

Though I cannot completely understand what it was like for Jesus, I do have some experience. In Maharashtra, we conducted a one-day healing meeting in a village area, and the Holy Spirit began to work powerfully. Several deaf people started hearing, and others were being instantly healed. At the end of the meeting, I stepped down from the small stage to pray for others one on one, and the crowd violently pressed toward me to touch me. I actually started to become frightened as they were pushing each other over and grabbing and pulling me. I had nowhere to go. I was surrounded! My friends immediately pulled me back up on stage.

Jesus developed such a deep relationship with the Holy Spirit that at the slightest move of His presence and power, Jesus was aware.

It wasn't a pleasant experience. That crowd was only two or three hundred people, but Jesus's crowd had thousands to tens of thousands.

Back to the story. Imagine you are pressing through the crowd following Jairus to his home. You hear your name being yelled out, people are touching your body, and others are holding onto you. The only security personnel you have are your disciples. They are trying their best to keep the crowd off of you, but to no avail.

Where is your attention? What are you thinking about? If you are like me and a normal person, your entire focus would be on the crowd and how to get past them to arrive at Jairus' house before his daughter dies.

Jesus was not that way. His thoughts, attention, and affections were not on the crowd, but upon the Holy Spirit. Suddenly, power went out of Jesus's body. Jesus could feel the Holy Spirit begin to move, and He was also moved. He knew that the Holy Spirit touched someone. I can imagine Jesus saying, "Oh, precious Holy Spirit, I just felt Your presence and power. You touched someone. What did You do, My Love?" Then, the Holy Spirit, smiling, replied, "Ask the crowd who touched You."

Do you see the intimacy? Jesus developed such a deep relationship with the Holy Spirit that at the slightest move of His presence and power, Jesus was aware. You are aware of that which possesses your attention and affections. The more intimate you are, the more aware you are.

When Jesus asked His disciples, "Who touched Me?" they thought it was an absurd question. I can just imagine them thinking, "What? What did the Teacher ask? Who touched Him? Hundreds of people have already touched Him, and more are touching Him even now! What is He asking?" The disciples' entire attention and focus was on the crowd, not on the Spirit of God. Beloved, it is possible for us to have that deep kind of relationship with the Holy Spirit. In modeling this kind of deep intimacy, Jesus is giving us a special invitation to know the Spirit of God.

The Holy Spirit was crucial in every aspect of Jesus's life. The Holy Spirit told Jesus where to go and to whom to minister (Mark 1:35–39), who to disciple, and who to appoint (Mark 3:13–15); how to heal the sick and perform miracles (Mark 7:32–34; John 9:1–9); and what to say and teach (Luke 20:21–25; John 14:10). This is the reason Jesus had 100% success in everything He did.

> He who sins is of the devil, for the devil has been sinning from the beginning. To this end, the Son of God was revealed: that he might destroy the works of the devil.
>
> — 1 John 3:8

Jesus came for many reasons, and one of those was to destroy the works of the devil. Sickness, disease, death, sin, and demonic torment are the works that Jesus came to destroy. But He, by Himself, did not destroy these works. It was through the person of the Holy Spirit (Acts 10:38) that Jesus destroyed Satan's works.

> ...he who says he remains in Him ought himself also to walk just like He walked."
>
> — 1 John 2:6

Apostle John is exhorting us to walk just as Jesus walked on this earth. That means to not only live a pure, holy life of faith, loving God and others, but also to receive and walk in the power and presence of the Holy Spirit.

Because the church has lived in such compromise and unbelief, this goal seems impossible and unrealistic to many. Either we deeply repent for our lukewarm spiritual lives and trust God with all of our hearts until Jesus's life becomes our reality, or we make excuses to justify our powerless lives. Most leaders in the church have taken the second option. Some of those who accept the teachings in this chapter still make excuses for their lack, saying, "Jesus had the Spirit without measure. We have the Spirit in measure; therefore, we cannot do everything as Jesus did," referring to John 3:34. Such thinking contradicts what Jesus boldly said in the Gospel of John:

> "Most assuredly, I say to you, he who believes in Me, the works that I do, he will do also; and greater works than these he will do, because I go to My Father."
>
> — John 14:12

If it is impossible to receive the same measure of the Spirit that Jesus did, then John 14:12 is impossible. How are we suppose to do the same works, and even greater works, if we have less of the Spirit than He did? Beloved, we have a measure of the Spirit, but it is not God who restricts the limit of that measure. We are the ones who set that limit, according to our hunger for Him (Matthew 5:6).

In history, there have been many amazing men and women of God who walked in incredible measures of the Spirit of God, such as John G. Lake, Smith Wigglesworth, and others. I would like to talk for a moment about Katherine Kuhlman. She was a simple woman who didn't have any special gifts, as most leaders do today. She was not a talented worship leader, nor was she a gifted speaker. She really had nothing going for her except she had a great love for the Holy Spirit. He was everything to her. She had many large meetings that filled stadiums, and incredible miracles were witnessed. In some cities where her meetings lasted many days, several hospitals were emptied because of such incredible healing power.

Before and after the meetings, due to the large crowds, she had to come and leave through a back door. In one large hotel, she was escorted through the kitchen to the stage to avoid the crowd. But as she walked among the kitchen staff, without speaking a word, they immediately fell to their knees, repenting and crying out for the mercy of God. Another time, she was walking through the airport to catch her flight. As she passed by a lady in a wheelchair, the presence and power of God around Katherine struck the lady, and, rising up from the wheelchair, she was instantly healed.

The life of Jesus and these testimonies are an invitation to you. You are invited to walk with the Spirit just as they did. Hear His voice, let faith arise in your heart, and seek to know this precious Holy Spirit!

4

Partnership of the Holy Spirit

OBEYING HIS VOICE

One Thursday evening several years ago, I was praying to the Lord, and the next day, I was invited to minister at a healing meeting in a village outside of Varanasi, a city in northern India. I was excited and asked the Lord what I should preach. I waited in silence, but heard nothing. Some time passed and I reminded the Lord, "Lord, I want to preach and speak what You desire. Speak to me." In a moment, I saw a vision. In the vision, I was standing in front of about 90 people in a church hall. I saw myself preaching, but as though I were sitting in the audience. Within a few seconds, the vision became blurry and difficult to see. There seemed to be large pockets of blindness. The other areas were very blurred. I asked, "Lord, what are You showing me? I don't understand." Immediately, I heard the voice of the Spirit, saying, "There will be a woman in the meeting whose left eye is blind, just as you are now seeing in the vision. Pray for her before preaching the Word."

The entire length of the vision lasted only a few seconds, and the voice spoke very quickly. I opened my eyes and wrote on a paper, "woman with a blind left eye." I then closed my eyes and asked the Lord again what I should preach. I waited and saw another vision. In the vision was a woman who was wearing a red sari (a traditional Indian dress). She was opening and closing her mouth repeatedly. I did not understand, so I asked, "Lord, what is this? I don't understand this vision either." I did not hear a voice this time, but I saw a red light blink in the jawbone joint every time the woman opened and closed her mouth. In my spirit, I knew that this woman suffered from pain in her jaw joints. I opened my eyes and also noted that on the paper. I continued to ask the Lord on what I should share, and I received no leading at all.

Friday morning, I was traveling to the meeting, and I was very excited. Upon arriving, there were about 90 people in the meeting. After worship ended, I was given the microphone. I stood up and boldly said, "There is a woman here whose left eye is blind. God is going to heal you right now! Stand up!"

I looked around the hall and, to my surprise, no one stood up. I immediately became very nervous. The hall was dead quiet. All the people were staring at me, and I started to imagine their thoughts, "Who is this crazy guy?"

I waited a moment and then spoke again, this time with less confidence, "Okay, I believe there is a woman here whose left eye is blind. If so, please stand up." I explained how the eye was blind, just as I saw in the vision. I stood there for a few seconds and waited to give time for people to respond. Each second felt like minutes, and no one responded.

I began to sweat profusely. It was May, the hot season, and I was already sweating, but now it was pouring off of me. I became very insecure and thought, "What am I supposed to do now?" The dead silence and their staring only made me feel worse.

I mustered up enough strength to ask one more time. "Listen to me carefully, please. If there is any woman in this meeting whose left eye is blind, please, please stand up."

I stood there a few more seconds, and a woman near the back of the meeting said, "Oh, that is me! My left eye is blind!" I thought, "Why didn't you stand up earlier!?" As she stood up, I realized something very important. The place where she was sitting was the exact area where I saw myself preaching in the vision. She came forward, and I laid my hand on her eye and said, "In Jesus's name, I—"

Only that much prayer came out of my mouth before her blind eye was opened and she could see clearly. "I can see! I can see!" She joyfully cried.

My emotions became bold again. I felt vindicated after the stares of the people. I was so excited that I said, "There is at least one woman here whose jawbone joints are in pain, especially when she opens and closes her mouth." To my surprise, *three* ladies came forward, and the second I prayed, BAM! Each of them was instantly healed! It was the start of a wonderful healing meeting, in the early years of miracle ministry.

What is the Will of God?

> Let your Kingdom come, your will be done, as in heaven, so on earth.
>
> — Matthew 6:10

In this chapter, I want to share with you how we must partner with the Holy Spirit so heaven becomes the reality of earth. It was the Holy Spirit who showed me those visions and manifested the healing power of God. But, apart from my partnership, He did not move. Likewise, apart from His leading and power, there would have been no healings or miracles, no matter how hard I prayed or how long I could have fasted.

The will of God is His kingdom being established on earth. There is no sickness in heaven. There are no demons in heaven. There is no fear, torment, depression, poverty, or curse in His kingdom. Knowing the characteristics of the kingdom of God is crucial for partnership with the Holy Spirit.

The will of God is His kingdom being established on earth.

Jesus went about in all Galilee, teaching in their synagogues, preaching the Good News of the Kingdom, and healing every disease and every sickness among the people. The report about him went out into all Syria. They brought to him all who were sick, afflicted with various diseases and torments, possessed with demons, epileptics, and paralytics; and he healed them.

— Matthew 4:23–24

We learned from last chapter that Jesus performed all of His works as a man submitted to the Father empowered by the Holy Spirit. Jesus preached the good news of the kingdom of heaven. (Matthew the author used the word kingdom of "heaven." Mark used the term kingdom of "God." Both mean the same thing.) What message did Jesus preach? He preached the good news of the kingdom of heaven/God. The Holy Spirit confirmed His message with power and, consequently, the sick were healed and the demonized were delivered. Let us look at another scripture that will give us even more insight to the kingdom of heaven.

Then one possessed by a demon, blind and mute, was brought to him and he healed him, so that the blind and mute man both spoke and saw. All the multitudes were amazed and said, "Can this be the son of David?" But when the Pharisees heard it, they said, "This man does not cast out demons, except by Beelzebul, the prince of the demons." Knowing their thoughts, Jesus said to them, "Every kingdom divided against itself is brought to desolation, and every city or house divided against itself will not stand. If Satan casts out Satan, he is divided against himself. How then will his kingdom stand? If I by Beelzebul cast out demons, by whom do your children cast them out? Therefore, they will be your judges. But if I by the Spirit of God cast out demons, then God's Kingdom has come upon you."

— Matthew 12:22–28

This is a fascinating story. First of all, we can note that the person was blind and mute due to a demonic presence and power. It was through the casting out of a demon that the blind and mute both saw and spoke. Jesus replies to the absurd accusations of the Pharisees and explains what transpired in the spirit realm. Jesus Himself said that He cast out the demons by the Spirit of God. It was the Holy Spirit who actually evicted the demon, but the command was given by Jesus. The Holy Spirit, who evicted the demon, manifested the kingdom of God upon the afflicted, which resulted in physical healing. There are four crucial elements to learn from this story:

1. There are only two types of spirits: demonic spirits and the Holy Spirit. Demonic spirits have the power to manifest the kingdom of darkness, and the Holy Spirit is the power of God that manifests the kingdom of heaven.

2. There are only two kingdoms: the kingdom of heaven and the kingdom of darkness. These kingdoms are dependent upon the spirits.

3. Each kingdom manifests its fruit. In this scenario, the kingdom of darkness caused physical blindness and dumbness. The kingdom of heaven caused physical healing.

4. Authority was given to the spirits to operate in power. The blind, dumb man gave his authority to the demons (Proverbs 26:2, Lamentations 5:7). Jesus used His authority by commanding the demon to come out of the man and leave.

The Holy Spirit responded to Jesus's authority and evicted the demon spirit. In this way, the Holy Spirit manifested the kingdom of heaven. It was not until Jesus commanded the evil spirit to leave that the Holy Spirit evicted it; Jesus was dependent upon the Holy Spirit. The Holy Spirit did not evict demons prior to Jesus commanding them; the Holy Spirit was dependent upon Jesus. Let me share another testimony to further illustrate this:

I was in Delhi, speaking to a small church group on a Sunday evening. After preaching, I gave an opportunity for people to receive prayer for healing. A young lady, about 21 years of age, came up to me. Her face was gloomy, and she was very depressed and discouraged. Did you know that this is a manifestation of the kingdom of darkness? Emotions are often the fruits of the kingdom present within a person. The kingdom of heaven manifests joy, peace, and confident expectation. The kingdom of darkness manifests depression, hopelessness and fear. When this woman approached me, I asked her what was wrong and how I could pray for her. She told me she had been having constant abdominal pain every day for the past eight months. She had gone to several doctors and took medicine, but nothing had helped.

I had her place her hand on her stomach area. Then, I placed my hand on top of hers and began to pray, "In Jesus's name, Holy Spirit, I invite Your presence. Come. I speak to this pain, and I command it to leave." The moment I commanded, I noticed a change in her countenance. I asked her how she was. "Oh, oh, the pain is gone, I have no more pain!" She said, smiling. I smiled in return and told her she could go now, and off she went.

About ten minutes later, though, while I was praying for a few more people, she returned with the same depressed look. I asked what happened. She replied that the pain just came back. I thought it was strange that the pain immediately left and was back again. From my previous experiences, I thought it was an afflicting spirit, but before praying again, I asked her, "Eight months ago, when this pain started, did anything significant happen in your life, good or bad?"

She looked up at me, a little surprised, and said, "Well, yes. I was seven months pregnant with twins. All of a sudden, both of the twins died. The doctors gave me some medicine to force the dead twins out. Shortly after that time, the stomach pain started."

I thought for a moment that the medicine may have caused the pain. But then, how does the pain disappear and return again? Convinced it was an afflicting spirit, I turned to her and commanded, "You afflicting devil, I bind you in Jesus's name, and I command you to come out of her!"

After commanding, I asked her again how she was. No change whatsoever, and the pain continued. At this point, I made the wisest decision possible. I stepped to the side for a moment, and in a quiet voice, I asked, "Holy Spirit, I have no clue what I am to do. Please guide me."

As quickly as I finished praying, I saw a vision that lasted about three seconds. In my mind, I saw a blackboard that teachers use to teach in school. Then, a piece of chalk flew into the air by itself and wrote, "spirit of death." As soon as I saw this, it vanished. Without waiting a second longer, I turned toward her and yelled, "You spirit of death, I command you, come out of her now!"

Immediately, she bent over and began to cough very loudly. She coughed hard about nine times and then stood up. Her countenance began to change, and she said, "All the pain is now gone. Also, I felt something come out of me." She then turned joyful again. I stayed in that church for another hour, and just before leaving, I asked her how she was. She said she was completely healed.

Here are my thoughts and conclusion about this deliverance healing. The spirit of death, in some way that was not revealed to me, entered this woman and killed her twins. Remember, the devil comes to steal, kill, and destroy (John 10:10). After killing the unborn, it turned against her and began afflicting her. When I laid my hands on her and released healing power, the spirit became frightened by the power of the Holy Spirit and silently hid inside of her. After she was far away from me, the spirit again began to afflict. This is one reason why some people come to meetings and get healed, but then the sickness later comes back. The devil, who was the source of the affliction, was not cast out. The spirit of death was manifesting the kingdom of darkness, which resulted in the death of her unborn, pain in her body, and depression in her soul. When the kingdom of heaven was manifested—by my commanding through the guidance and power of the Holy Spirit—healing and joy were released.

In this deliverance healing, I did very little. But, it is important to note that the Holy Spirit did not move until I heard and obeyed.

The Holy Spirit gave revelation. I simply obeyed and commanded according to that revelation and then the Holy Spirit evicted the demon and manifested the kingdom of God. This is how we partner with the Holy Spirit.

> For God's Kingdom is not eating and drinking, but righteousness, peace, and joy in the Holy Spirit.
>
> — Romans 14:17

The kingdom of heaven is completely dependent upon the Holy Spirit and only manifests through Him. The Holy Spirit is the power of the kingdom. But, there is a difference between power and authority. Upon this earth, God has given us the authority to fulfill His will. God, apart from our partnership, will not fulfill His will upon this earth. This is our responsibility. Note the following verses.

INCREDIBLE AUTHORITY, IMMENSE RESPONSIBILITY

> The heavens are the heavens of Yahweh; but the earth He has given to the children of men.
>
> — Psalm 115:16

> I will give to you the keys of the Kingdom of Heaven, and whatever you bind on earth will have been bound in heaven; and whatever you release on earth will have been released in heaven.
>
> — Matthew 16:19

> Let your Kingdom come. Let your will be done, as in heaven, so on earth.
>
> — Matthew 6:10

The earth was given to men to steward and rule. God gave us the keys, which represent authority, of the kingdom of heaven. That authority rests on us. We are the mediators between heaven and earth, the channel that God has chosen. That is why God has commanded us to pray with authority to manifest His kingdom. Therefore, the manifestation of His kingdom on earth, and seeing His will accomplished on earth, is our responsibility.

But, authority without power is limited. For example, let's say a policeman witnessed from a distance a thief stealing a woman's purse. The policeman yells at the thief, "Stop! I, by my authority, command your arrest!" But, the thief looks the policeman over and finds that he does not have a gun, a baton, or any weapon whatsoever. Because the policeman lacks power, the thief might be emboldened to run away or even fight the officer. The policeman has the government-given authority to arrest and maintain order, but without power, such as a gun, to enforce that authority, he will be of minimal use.

Here is another example. A contractor buys some land and employs a team. The team's responsibility is to lay the foundation and erect a building to the 10th floor. The contractor and the team have all the permits from the governing authorities to build, but there is a problem. The contractor and the team don't have the equipment necessary: no bulldozer or heavy machinery.

You can see that authority apart from power is very ineffective. In the same way, God's people are trying to establish His kingdom here on earth, but without power, very little of heaven is visible on this earth.

Those who God sends carry God's authority. God sent Jesus to earth to rule and reign, but the kingdom did not manifest through Jesus until He received the Holy Spirit (Luke 3:21–22, 4:14). Jesus never tried to use His authority without power. Jesus then sent us out to do the same works that He did (Matthew 28:18–19, Mark 16:15–18, John 20:21), and in sending us out, He gave us His authority. But, Jesus warned us to wait until we receive power before we use that authority.

He said to them, "Thus it is written, and thus it was necessary for the Christ to suffer and to rise from the dead the third day, and that repentance and remission of sins should be preached in His name to all the nations, beginning at Jerusalem. You are witnesses of these things. Behold, I send out the promise of my Father on you. But wait in the city of Jerusalem until you are clothed with power from on high."

— Luke 24:46–49

But you will receive power when the Holy Spirit has come upon you. You will be witnesses to me in Jerusalem, in all Judea and Samaria, and to the uttermost parts of the earth.

— Acts 1:8

COMMON MISCONCEPTIONS

The Holy Spirit, apart from us operating by this authority that has been given to us, will not act. This is where many believers have peculiar thinking. They say, "Well, if God wants to do something, He will! God doesn't need me!" It is true that God doesn't need us. But, He desires our partnership so much that He freely placed restrictions upon Himself so that apart from our loving obedience, His will is not accomplished on this earth.

At this point, I need to address a very critical point of theology that can greatly hinder our walk with the Lord. Many Christians accept an unbiblical view of God's sovereignty. In essence, many believe that whatever God's will is, it will be accomplished independently from all other factors. The evidence of this false belief is everywhere.

For example, there was a man my relatives knew who became sick with cancer. Being a Christian, he believed that God was going to heal him. Relatives and friends called him and said, "Don't worry! God will heal you!" They also prayed for him. In the end, this man died. All the believers and relatives made comments like, "Well, we believed, but it obviously was not God's will," or, "What else can we do? Life and death are in God's hands," and even, "The will of God is very mysterious." I attended the funeral of a young Christian boy who died of rabies. Sad to say, he suffered a horrible death. At the funeral, the pastor, in trying to comfort the family, said, "Life and death are in God's hands. We cannot always understand His mysterious will. God so loved this boy that He took him at an early age." These are all demonic lies that give excuse to the powerlessness of the Christian community.

> *Jesus healed every sick person who came to Him, delivered every tormented person who cried out for His help, and comforted every person whose heart was broken.*

Let me tell you something that liberated me. I do not get my faith, hope, and trust from assumptions, traditions, or from twisted doctrines of the Bible. I get my theology from the life of Jesus Christ. He only did what pleased the Father (John 5:19–20, 6:38, 14:8–11). Every word Jesus spoke, every action He undertook, and every miracle He performed was the perfect will of the Father. Jesus is the perfect representation of God (Hebrews 1:1–3). Did Jesus ever make anyone sick? Did Jesus ever say to a sick person, "It is not my will to heal you," or, "This sickness is an instrument to make you more righteous and holy," or, "Fast and pray until you deeply repent of your sins, and then I will heal you"? No. Jesus healed every sick person who came to Him, delivered every tormented person who cried out for His help, and comforted every person whose heart was broken.

My faith is not based upon what happens or what does not happen. I do not allow circumstances to dictate what I believe. My faith is based strictly upon the life of Jesus, and that is why I see miracles, such as the deaf hearing, the blind seeing, tumors dissolving, and the crippled walking. Jesus said, "He who believes in ME will do the same works that I do." Our faith must be in Him and Him alone if we are to expect the Holy Spirit to manifest the kingdom of God powerfully through our lives. If the will of God is not being fulfilled in our lives or in a situation, then you can basically conclude that we are not (1) walking in the revelation of our authority, (2) not receiving the proper revelation or guidance from the Holy Spirit for that specific situation, or (3) and we are unable to apply His presence and power.

Now, we must understand our partnership with the Holy Spirit. Read the following verses.

> When the Counselor has come, whom I will send to you from the Father, the Spirit of truth, who proceeds from the Father, He will testify about me. You will also testify, because you have been with me from the beginning.
>
> — John 15:26–27

> But you will receive power when the Holy Spirit has come upon you. You will be witnesses to me in Jerusalem, in all Judea and Samaria, and to the uttermost parts of the earth.
>
> — Acts 1:8

> God exalted Him with his right hand to be a Prince and a Savior, to give repentance to Israel and remission of sins. We are His witnesses of these things, and so also is the Holy Spirit, whom God has given to those who obey Him.
>
> — Acts 5:31–32

We must understand an important truth, that there are only two types of witnesses on this earth: the Holy Spirit and us. We have been given the task to testify of the life, death, and resurrection of Jesus Christ. Jesus and the Father are both seated in heaven. Why are they seated? Because their work is done and they are waiting on us. But, the Holy Spirit was poured out on earth (Acts 2:33). We are eagerly waiting for Jesus to return (Philippians 3:20), but the Holy Spirit is here, right now. The Holy Spirit is waiting for us to partner with Him and to testify of Jesus.

How does this partnership work? It works best when we get to know each other intimately. Miracles happen when we receive guidance from the Holy Spirit in a specific situation. We act according to that guidance in authority. Then, the Holy Spirit, whom we have honored and obeyed, will manifest the kingdom of heaven. If there are no miracles happening or spiritual gifts operating in our midst, we must question if the Holy Spirit is even present and if we can hear His voice.

PRACTICAL EXAMPLES OF PARTNERSHIP

He said to them, "Go into all the world, and preach the Good News to the whole creation."

— Mark 16:15

"When he has come, he will convict the world about sin, about righteousness, and about judgment; about sin, because they don't believe in me; about righteousness, because I am going to my Father, and you won't see me any more; about judgment, because the prince of this world has been judged."

— John 16:8–11

We are given the task of preaching the Gospel, but our words alone will never convict or transform a sinner. If the Holy Spirit is present when the Gospel is preached, sinners often weep, shake, see visions, fall over, get delivered from demons, or are healed. Such manifestations are normal when the Holy Spirit is present. The greater His presence is during the preaching of the Gospel, the more manifestations occur. Without the work of the Spirit, our preaching is in vain. But, the Holy Spirit does not usually move until we preach. The more He is present, the more effective the Gospel message will be.

"These signs will accompany those who believe: in my name they will cast out demons; they will speak with new languages."

— Mark 16:17

"Heal the sick, cleanse the lepers, and cast out demons. Freely you received, so freely give."

— Matthew 10:8

"But if I by the Spirit of God cast out demons, then God's Kingdom has come upon you."

— Matthew 12:28

We are given instructions by Jesus to cast out demons. This is the first sign listed for those who are walking in true faith and partnership with the Holy Spirit. We must understand that we give the command, but the Holy Spirit evicts the demon spirit. We can command demons to leave all day long (Acts 19:14–17), but not until the Holy Spirit manifests in power will the demons leave.

I have noticed over the years of healing the sick and casting out demons that to the degree the Holy Spirit's presence is manifesting, that same degree of delivering and healing power is present. That is, the greater His presence is, the easier it is to cast out demons. Of all the healings and miracles I have witnessed, about 50% of them were accomplished by the evicting of a demon. I will give a remarkable story to explain this.

For many years, the Lord has given me the privilege of going to Maharashtra to teach leaders and conduct miracle meetings. Many years ago, I met a lady who was about 40 years of age named Rajjubai. She was the most visibly demon-tormented person I have ever met. She came to several of my meetings seeking deliverance. For 20 years, demons tormented her by suddenly manifesting in her body. She would fall on the ground, convulse, scream, shake, and lay unconscious for hours. When the demons would manifest, you could see an invisible force twisting her arms and attacking her body. It was horrible to witness. From years of this torment, her entire right arm became paralyzed; she was unable to lift it up or use it for any work. Her face was also permanently distorted and damaged, as if a wild animal attacked her. She said that her face was continually in pain. These demonic attacks would suddenly happen in prayer meetings, church services, or any large convention. This was not just at places of worship. Even at home, demons would randomly manifest in her. These manifestations were so dramatic that her own children feared her and would always run to their father if they had any needs.

Rajjubai came to two of my meetings, and I saw her manifesting for hours during the worship, preaching, and ministry time. I personally prayed for her on several occasions, but to no avail. She was known in the area as the woman who no minister could deliver. Thank God she didn't give up hope! Year after year she continually sought Jesus and received prayer, though it looked futile.

In May 2012, I was invited to be the main speaker at an All Maharashtra Pastors and Leaders Conference in Ahmednagar. The evening miracle meetings were open to the public, and we had crowds of 1,500 to 2,000 people. Rajjubai was also there, and I saw her again rolling on the ground being tormented by devils. The third and final night of the meeting, before preaching, the Holy Spirit spoke to me, saying, "Tonight I want you to preach on the resurrection of Jesus and His complete victory over Satan and all darkness. Then, call up all those who are demonized to the front for prayer."

It was a wonderful time of ministering the word, and as the Holy Spirit instructed me, I called up all those who were in any degree tormented by demons. A large number of people came up to the stage. I then proceeded to invite the presence of the Holy Spirit and with authority began to rebuke, bind, and command the demons to leave. Many immediately fell to the ground screaming, convulsing, and manifesting vividly. During the message, there was a strong presence of the Lord, but during prayer, it dramatically increased.

As is our custom, after prayer we invite those healed and delivered to come up on stage to testify. Many were in line, but I saw Rajjubai also in line! I asked my wife to personally check her to see what happened. When it was Rajjubai's turn, she shared how she was tormented for years and was now delivered. I asked, "How do you know you are now delivered?" She explained that during the mass prayer, a powerful presence from heaven fell on her, expelling the demons. Her arms and face were completely healed at that same moment. She also felt incredible peace and lightness throughout her body. Not only Rajjubai, but many others who were tormented for many years were instantly delivered.

I was so happy and joyful, but the movement of the Spirit didn't stop there! After testimonies, we usually dismiss the crowd and pray for as many as we can who still need a breakthrough. An unusual presence of the Holy Spirit continued to rest on me. Many sick people were in line for prayer, and if the source of the disease was a demon, then the moment I laid my hands on them, they would immediately manifest. This had happened occasionally during the years, but an exceptional anointing was upon me at that moment. Person after person screamed, fell to the ground, and began shaking. As the demon left, they were instantly healed! There was such a contrast between this meeting and the many previous prayers for deliverance that had ended without success. I learned that He, the Holy Spirit, is the key for freedom.

> ...they will take up serpents; and if they drink any deadly thing, it will in no way hurt them; they will lay hands on the sick, and they will recover.
>
> — Mark 16:18

The healing of the sick is very similar to the casting out of demons. We act in faith, and the Holy Spirit responds to that faith and ministers healing power. We are commanded to lay hands on the sick. Obviously, we cannot heal the sick. We do not possess the power to do such a thing. The power that destroys sickness and heals the body is the person of the Holy Spirit. Laying on of hands is not the only way healing is administered, but it is one of the major methods. I have noticed that in many circumstances, until I lay my hands on the sick, the Holy Spirit will not heal. Sometimes during prayer, I will hear the voice of the Holy Spirit say, "Lay your hands there, now." As I lay my hands there, His presence flows, and healing manifests. Does God need me to lay hands on the sick? Absolutely not. God doesn't need me to do anything for Him to act. But, to perfect the beauty of partnership and to continue dancing with the Holy Spirit according to the rhythm of heaven, He wants us to do something. We are not called as an audience to watch in awe of what God does. Rather, we are called to His side, to be a part of every magnificent miracle He performs.

I have been in meetings where empty hands are laid on people and nothing happens. No healing, no impartation, no change in anyone's life. At those times, we are not walking according to the presence and voice of the Holy Spirit. If we are led by Him and are filled with His presence, laying on of hands is an incredibly fun and amazing experience, in both giving and receiving!

> For he who speaks in another language speaks not to men, but to God; for no one understands; but in the Spirit he speaks mysteries.
>
> — 1 Corinthians 14:2

Speaking in heavenly tongues is a common miracle that is dependent upon the Holy Spirit. Speaking in tongues requires the ability of the Holy Spirit (Acts 2:4). In most circumstances, it is when we open our mouth and begin to speak that the Holy Spirit give us utterance. We choose to open our mouths and in faith, speak. Then, the Holy Spirit responds by giving us utterance. Many people say to me, "I want to speak in tongues, so I am just waiting on the Holy Spirit to make me speak. When He wants me to, He will force me." Though at certain times the Holy Spirit so inspires someone to speak that it feels beyond their control and words flow out of their mouth, this is an exception. Most of the time, we feel an impression to speak, a "bubbling" in our gut and/or faith, and we act.

The Father, in His great wisdom and pleasure, designed this unique partnership and gave us the greatest promise of all, His Holy Spirit. (Luke 24:49). God will not scrap this plan and start "plan B" for us if we are too ignorant or refuse to walk with the Holy Spirit. Through this partnership, God's kingdom will transform the nations (Matthew 24:14), and the knowledge of His glory will cover the earth as the waters cover the seas (Habakkuk 2:14).

5

Baptism of the Holy Spirit

THE PURPOSE OF WATER BAPTISM

In this chapter, I want to teach on what the baptism of the Holy Spirit is, its purpose, and how to receive it. We must first understand what water baptism is and how the baptism of the Holy Spirit differs in purpose and results. Let's look at the following scriptures.

> He said to them, "Go into all the world, and preach the Good News to the whole creation. He who believes and is baptized will be saved; but he who disbelieves will be condemned."
>
> — Mark 16:15–16

> Go, and make disciples of all nations, baptizing them in the name of the Father and of the Son and of the Holy Spirit.
>
> — Matthew 28:19

> In those days, John the Baptizer came, preaching in the wilderness of Judea, saying, 'Repent, for the Kingdom of Heaven is at hand!' ... They were baptized by him in the Jordan, confessing their sins... 'I indeed baptize you in water for repentance, but he who comes after me is mightier than I, whose shoes I am not worthy to carry. He will baptize you in the Holy Spirit.'"
>
> — Matthew 3:1–2, 6, 11

In the above verses, we can see that water baptism is directly related to faith and repentance. Faith, repentance, confession, and baptism are the first steps in our salvation walk, and we can always link these four necessary acts together.

Faith is a by-product of the revealing work of the Holy Spirit (John 16:8–11, 1 Corinthians 12:3). Remember that everything we have or do is a response to grace. The Holy Spirit graciously reveals Jesus to us, and accepting that revelation is faith. Rejecting that revelation is unbelief. Apart from the revealing work of the Holy Spirit, no one can believe and be saved (1 Corinthians 2:14). Saving faith is trusting in the nature and work of Jesus, as He died for our sins and was raised from the dead (Romans 10:9). Not only does the Holy Spirit reveal to us the life, death, and resurrection of Jesus, but also our sins, convicting us of evil. This is where repentance comes in.

To repent, in the Greek, means to "change the way you think." If we change the way we think, we inevitably change our behavior and the direction of our lives. The Holy Spirit is the power of God in our lives. He gives us the ability to repent. Repentance is a gift of God (Acts 5:31, 11:18, 2 Corinthians 7:10, 2 Timothy 2:25). Responding to the convicting work of the Holy Spirit is repentance. As we change the way we think, the Holy Spirit empowers us to walk in that renewed mind. He convicts of sin and is the One who empowers us to walk in freedom.

Upon receiving the revelation of Jesus as Lord and Savior and being deeply convicted of our sins, confession is the next necessary step. In John's baptism, people confessed their sins as they were baptized in water (Matthew 3:6). For saving faith to take full effect, confessing Jesus as Lord and Savior is essential (Romans 10:9, 1 Timothy 1:1). All true heart-based confession is a by-product of the Holy Spirit's inner work (1 Corinthians 12:3).

Finally, after faith, repentance, and confession, one takes the step of water baptism. The reason for water baptism should be to please God and to come into agreement with our new identity in Christ. Obedience pleases God. Anyone who is being convicted and led of the Holy Spirit should be water baptized.

I would like to give a practical example. Say I came to Delhi to live, and I am looking for an apartment. Upon finding an owner, I talk with him and get to know him over chai. Then, he discusses with me the agreement of living in his apartment. He requires that I use the apartment for only residential purposes, pay a monthly rent fee of 10,000 rupees, and I would be responsible for the electricity bills and all maintenance. He promises to

The reason for water baptism should be to please God and to come into agreement with our new identity in Christ.

supply water and install fans and a water heater. I then tell him that I agree and would like to rent his apartment. Later, the owner makes a lease agreement outlining the conditions above. We both agree by signing the agreement. But, one final step is still necessary. The agreement needs to be notarized by a government official to have any lasting legal grounds. In the same way, knowing the person and work of Jesus is faith. Willingness and agreement to live according to His commandments and truth is repentance. A verbal agreement to proceed further is confession. Finally, water baptism is the heavenly notary that seals our agreement with the Lord Jesus Christ. The Holy Spirit Himself is that seal (Ephesians 1:13–14).

We must understand that the Holy Spirit is responsible for the work of salvation in our lives. So, how is our relationship with the Holy Spirit established? Once we respond to the work of the Holy Spirit with living faith, repentance, confession, and water baptism, the Holy Spirit begins to live inside of us. I would like to add that there are many true, repentant believers who have not yet taken water baptism, either by ignorance or other reasons, in whom the Holy Spirit already lives. The Holy Spirit is not legalistic. By teaching faith, repentance, confession, and water baptism for salvation, I am not teaching legalism, but rather the way the Bible instructs us to walk. If you are walking in true faith in Jesus, but have not been water baptized, I do not condemn you, but I do urge you to immediately obey God. Water baptism is one important and necessary step for believers to outwardly identify with the new inner life graciously provided for in the cross and resurrection (Romans 6:3–8, Colossians 2:11–13). Note the following verses in their relation to the Holy Spirit:

> Peter said to them, "Repent, and be baptized, every one of you, in the name of Jesus Christ for the forgiveness of sins, and you will receive the gift of the Holy Spirit."
>
> — Acts 2:38

> But you are not in the flesh but in the Spirit, if it is so that the Spirit of God dwells in you. But if any man doesn't have the Spirit of Christ, he is not His. The Spirit himself testifies with our spirit that we are children of God.
>
> — Romans 8:9, 16

> Or don't you know that your body is a temple of the Holy Spirit which is in you, which you have from God? You are not your own, for you were bought with a price. Therefore, glorify God in your body and in your spirit, which are God's.
>
> — 1 Corinthians 6:19–20

> By this we know that we remain in Him and He in us, because He has given us of His Spirit."
>
> — 1 John 4:13

> That good thing which was committed to you, guard through the Holy Spirit who dwells in us.
>
> — 2 Timothy 1:14

Upon believing and receiving Jesus Christ as our Lord and Savior, we realize we are adopted as God's children (John 1:12, Galatians 4:5–6), and we are immediately given the most precious gift of all, the person of the Holy Spirit. Upon saving faith, the Holy Spirit comes and lives inside of us. This is very important to note, that He lives inside of us. The Holy Spirit lives inside of us for our personal needs, to connect and commune with the Father and the Son, and to walk according to the will of God.

Some believers who have received the baptism of the Holy Spirit judge other believers who do not have the evidence of the baptism of the Holy Spirit, by saying, "You do not have the Spirit of God." This is a horrible, false understanding of the Word of God. Any true believer in Jesus Christ has the Holy Spirit living inside of them.

The Purpose of the Baptism in the Holy Spirit

So, what is the baptism of the Holy Spirit? The baptism of the Holy Spirit is when the Holy Spirit comes upon a believer for the ministry to others. With a commission to serve others comes the power to fulfill that commission, and that is exactly what the baptism of the Spirit is. A simple way to say it is: The Holy Spirit is in me, for me, and upon me for others.

Let's look to the ministry of Jesus and the apostles. When reading the following scriptures, note the words "on" and "upon."

> Now when all the people were baptized, Jesus also had been baptized and was praying. The sky was opened, and the Holy Spirit descended in a bodily form like a dove on Him; and a voice came out of the sky, saying "You are my beloved Son. In you, I am well pleased." Jesus returned in the power of the Spirit into Galilee, and news about Him spread through all the surrounding area. "The Spirit of the Lord is on Me, because he has anointed Me to preach good news to the poor. He has sent Me to heal the broken hearted, to proclaim release to the captives, recovering of sight to the blind, to deliver those who are crushed."

> — Luke 3:21–22, 4:14, 4:18

Behold, my servant whom I have chosen; my beloved in whom my soul is well pleased: I will put my Spirit on Him. He will proclaim justice to the nations.

— Matthew 12:18

I didn't recognize Him, but He who sent me to baptize in water, He said to me, "On whomever you will see the Spirit descending, and remaining on Him, the same is He who baptizes in the Holy Spirit.'"

— John 1:33

But you will receive power when the Holy Spirit has come upon you. You will be witnesses to Me in Jerusalem, in all Judea and Samaria, and to the uttermost parts of the earth.

— Acts 1:8

It will be in the last days, says God, that I will pour out My Spirit on all flesh. Your sons and your daughters will prophesy. Your young men will see visions. Your old men will dream dreams. Yes, and on My servants and on My handmaidens in those days, I will pour out My Spirit, and they will prophesy."

— Acts 2:17–18

Notice it doesn't say the Holy Spirit came inside Jesus or inside the apostles, but came on them. In each reference to the Holy Spirit coming upon, there was a commissioning for a specific work that was impossible apart from the power of the Holy Spirit. The presence of the Holy Spirit upon someone is evidence of the commission of heaven. The apostles received power to be witnesses—the kind that, through the power of the Holy Spirit, cause the blind to see, the deaf to hear, the cripple to walk, and demons to flee (Matthew 11:5, 15:30–31, Acts 5:14–16). The Gospel was always intended to be accompanied with signs, wonders, and miracles (Mark 16:17–20, 1 Corinthians 2:4–5, 1 Thessalonians 1:5). It was never word alone, but word with power (1 Corinthians 4:20). Every believer who is truly baptized in the Spirit will have power to be a witness of Christ.

The baptism of the Holy Spirit is intended to make us powerful witnesses of the life, death, and resurrection of Jesus, and to empower us to love others by destroying the works of the devil. Therefore, it is necessary that one be surrendered to the calling and service of God to receive this baptism. This is a submersion, not in water, but in the person, presence, and power of the Holy Spirit. When we take water baptism, we agree in faith that we are united to Christ in His death and resurrection and, consequently, walk in a new way of life (Romans 6:3–4). The baptism of the Holy Spirit is to be covered, smeared, and anointed with His power for His purposes.

Lets now look at the following scriptures and note the results of the baptism of the Holy Spirit.

> But you will receive power when the Holy Spirit has come upon you. You will be witnesses to me in Jerusalem, in all Judea and Samaria, and to the uttermost parts of the earth."
>
> — Acts 1:8

The evidence of the baptism of the Holy Spirit is power to be a supernatural witness of Jesus.

> Now when the day of Pentecost had come, they were all with one accord in one place. Suddenly, there came from the sky a sound like the rushing of a mighty wind, and it filled all the house where they were sitting. Tongues like fire appeared and were distributed to them, and one sat on each of them. They were all filled with the Holy Spirit and began to speak with other languages, as the Spirit gave them the ability to speak. But Peter, standing up with the eleven, lifted up his voice, and spoke out to them, "You men of Judea, and all you who dwell at Jerusalem, let this be known to you, and listen to my words... Let all the house of Israel therefore know certainly that God has made Him both Lord and Christ, this Jesus whom you crucified."
>
> — Acts 2:1–4, 14, 36

Those baptized experienced the presence and power of the Holy Spirit, and they spoke in tongues. Also, Peter, who was so afraid of those who crucified Jesus that he denied Him three times, became so emboldened and fearless that he preached the Gospel openly to them.

> "While Peter was still speaking these words, the Holy Spirit fell on all those who heard the word. They of the circumcision who believed were amazed, as many as came with Peter, because the gift of the Holy Spirit was also poured out on the Gentiles. For they heard them speaking in other languages and magnifying God."
>
> — Acts 10:44–46

> "When Paul had laid his hands on them, the Holy Spirit came on them, and they spoke with other languages and prophesied."
>
> — Acts 19:6

Again, we see the manifestation of the gift of tongues, unique Spirit-led worship, and the gift of prophecy.

In Chapters 6 and 7, we will learn in detail how the power and the gifts of the Holy Spirit are essential for the establishment of the kingdom of God upon earth. But now, we are going to see who is able to receive the baptism of the Holy Spirit.

RECEIVING THE SPIRIT BAPTISM

Let's begin with the following scriptures to consider:

> "It will be in the last days," says God, "that I will pour out My Spirit on all flesh. Your sons and your daughters will prophesy. Your young men will see visions. Your old men will dream dreams. Yes, and on my servants and on my handmaidens in those days, I will pour out my Spirit, and they will prophesy."
>
> — Acts 2:17–18

The Spirit of truth, whom the world can't receive; for it doesn't see Him, neither knows Him. You know Him, for He lives with you, and will be in you.

— John 14:17

The Spirit of the Lord is on Me, because he has anointed Me to preach good news to the poor. He has sent Me to heal the broken hearted, to proclaim release to the captives, recovering of sight to the blind, to deliver those who are crushed, and to proclaim the acceptable year of the Lord.

— Luke 4:18–19

God desires to pour out the baptism of the Holy Spirit upon all believers. There are two requisites for anyone to receive the baptism of the Holy Spirit:

1. The person must be a genuine believer in Jesus Christ.

2. The person must be surrendered to the service and calling of God.

The baptism of the Spirit is not for our personal enjoyment, nor for the selfish growth of our church and ministries, nor to make us feel good about ourselves. This baptism is strictly for the service of others (1 Corinthians 12:7). Now that we covered the requisites, let us look to see how we can practically receive it.

I tell you, keep asking, and it will be given you. Keep seeking, and you will find. Keep knocking, and it will be opened to you. For everyone who asks receives. He who seeks finds. To him who knocks it will be opened. Which of you fathers, if your son asks for bread, will give him a stone? Or if he asks for a fish, he won't give him a snake instead of a fish, will he? Or if he asks for an egg, he won't give him a scorpion, will he? If you then, being evil, know how to give good gifts to your children, how much more will your heavenly Father give the Holy Spirit to those who ask him?

— Luke 11:9–13

Blessed are those who hunger and thirst after righteousness, for they shall be filled.

— Matthew 5:6

I have found through the years that faith and hunger for God are the two greatest keys to receiving anything from Him. Spiritual hunger attracts the attention, presence, and hand of God, just as a magnet attracts metal to itself. In the same way, apathy and indifference repel the presence of God away from us, because when we harbor such emotions, we are judging Him worthless. Hunger alone, though, is not sufficient to receive. Faith is the spirit-man's ability to receive that which has already been perceived as God's will. In any place where I have witnessed or experienced genuine hunger and faith, God has always responded. Our hunger and faith may be tested for a season, but it will always attract the invasion of God. If you are truly hungry for the baptism of the Holy Spirit and have faith to receive, you are inches away from the experience. You just need to act upon that faith.

My First Experience of the Baptism in the Holy Spirit

I would like to share my own story. When I was 19 years of age, I was a new believer and was very zealous for the Lord. I became friends with a lady who went to my church, and her daughter and I were friends in high school. Her name was Susan Waddell. I would spend many hours at her place learning from her. Being new to the church, I slowly came to know that they believed in the Holy Spirit and His gifts. Since our church was not very charismatic in demonstrating the gifts, I had very little understanding of how they worked. Susan gave me a book that explained about the baptism of the Holy Spirit and the gifts of the Spirit. As I read through the book, my spirit began to realize that there was a new world of the Spirit that I was unaware of. I began to greatly hunger for this baptism and the gifts. As I read the book, I came to realize that this was a supernatural experience that could not be made up; God was going to touch me in a tangible and supernatural way.

Though prior to reading this book, I would weep strongly at the sweet love of God, and I saw visions on a few occasions, I had still not experienced the fire, power, and presence of the Holy Spirit explained in the book. I was very excited and hungry, but I was uncertain as to how this was going to happen. How was I supposed to speak in another language I never knew before? What was going to happen when the Holy Spirit descended upon me? The unknown made me very anxious, and I felt butterflies in my stomach.

One afternoon, after reading 2/3 of the book, I called Susan from work and told her that I needed the baptism of the Holy Spirit. I didn't want to wait another day! Before leaving work and arriving at her home, I was very nervous, even to the point of shaking. Susan welcomed me into her home and prepared a group of her friends to pray with me. She bought me pizza, but I was so excited and nervous that I was unable to eat even one bite. I sat down on the living room floor, and they made a circle and sat around me. They placed their hands on me and began to quietly pray over me in tongues.

I prayed within my spirit, "Father God, I want the baptism of the Holy Spirit. I don't even entirely understand what I am about to receive, but I know it is from You. I want all that You will give me. I don't even know how I am supposed to speak in tongues. You fill me with Your Holy Spirit."

I prayed within my spirit, "Father God, I want the baptism of the Holy Spirit. I don't even entirely understand what I am about to receive, but I know it is from You. I want all that You will give me. I don't even know how I am supposed to speak in tongues. You fill me with Your Holy Spirit."

As I was in the middle of prayer, I felt a strong bolt of electricity flow into my body. It felt like it entered in through my hands, and my whole body jerked. The power was so strong that my friend who was sitting directly in front of me fell backwards. What I am about to describe to you is difficult to say in words. I felt like my spirit left my body and was present with God's thick presence in heaven. Though I could see only a brilliant bright light, I felt the greatest measure of joy, peace, and love that I had ever experienced up to that time. I was about 95% conscious of this heavenly realm and only about 5% conscious of the earthly realm where I was sitting. While in this heavenly state, I could hear someone speaking extremely fast in an unknown language from the earthly realm. My spirit thought, "Who is that?" As soon as I asked the question within myself, I realized that it was my body who was speaking in tongues!

Then, within a split second, my spirit returned to my body. I didn't even know what I was saying, but it was flowing out of my mouth like a gushing river. When I became fully conscious of my physical being, the flow of tongues stopped and I came to myself. I was overwhelmed by the experience! Those who sat there and watched me said that I spoke in tongues much longer than I thought. My time in the heavenly realm felt like less than five seconds, but it was much, much longer in actual time on the earth. My being was so full of joy, peace, and love that I could not even express it or describe it in words. If someone offered me a million dollars, it would have seemed like dirt compared to what I had just experienced.

After rejoicing, I got in my car and began to drive back home. I was so thankful, but a little confused. As I watched others speak in tongues, I noticed that they spoke as they desired. But during my experience, I was not in control at all. How was I supposed to speak in tongues again, if I desired? I asked the Lord, and upon asking Him, several strange words and sentences came to my mind of an unknown language. I began to speak those words over and over, and as I did, I received even more words in tongues, until I could speak fluently. Also, the gift of prophecy began to bloom in my life as I started to see many visions and prophesy over others. It was the beautiful start of an adventure with the Holy Spirit.

You must understand that the baptism of the Holy Spirit is the beginning of a new walk with the Holy Spirit, a partnership for the furtherance of the Gospel. It is not an end, but a beginning. Over the years, I have met people and asked them, "Have you been baptized in the Holy Spirit?" "Yes, that was over 20 years ago," they replied. "Since then, what has happened in your life?" I asked. "Ahhhh... not much..." I often hear. Many people believe that receiving the baptism is an end. They may say, "I spoke in tongues, I got it!" What they fail to realize is that's only the beginning of knowing the Holy Spirit in a deep way and partnering with Him to establish the Kingdom of God on earth.

Before we move on, I'd like to take a moment to address a potential area of confusion: various terms and meanings. The term, "baptism of the Holy Spirit" (Acts 1:5), is equal to and means the same thing as "the outpouring of the Holy Spirit" (Acts 2:17), "being filled with the Holy Spirit" (Acts 2:4), and "receiving the Holy Spirit" (Acts 8:17). They are all terms that mean the same thing, and the effect is the same, which is the empowerment of the Holy Spirit for the purpose of the ministry to others.

An Increased Measure of the Spirit

It is important to note that the apostles were "filled with the Spirit" multiple times. I believe the empowerment of the Holy Spirit is not a single event in our lives, but can be received again and again. Accordingly, the apostles were first baptized and filled with the Holy Spirit in Acts 2:4. But, we see in Acts 4:31 and 33 that the apostles were filled again with the Holy Spirit, which resulted in "great power" and "great grace." They received a measure of the Holy Spirit the first time, and that measure increased in Acts 4:33 with the second filling of the Holy Spirit.

I have also experienced this "refilling" of the Holy Spirit that resulted in greater power and grace upon my life. Many, many years after my initial baptism of the Holy Spirit, I was very hungry and desperate for more of God. That hunger led me to Redding, California, to a church called Bethel. The Bethel Church Sunday service was already packed when I arrived, and I found a seat near the very back. There were about two thousand people present.

After worship, I was listening to Pastor Bill Johnson preach. Pastor Bill was preaching well, but slowly and peacefully. At one point, he stopped in the middle of his message and stood there. The room was very quiet, and each passing second felt like a minute. While staring at him, I began to think, "What happened? Did he forget his own message?" After a few more seconds, he began to touch the side of his stomach. The room was pin drop silent, I thought, "Does he have gas or what? Why is he touching the side of his stomach?" Then, he pointed to the side of the room where I was seated and said, "I believe there is a woman seated in this section towards the back. You have a stomach tumor on this side. Stand up, God wants to heal you." A few rows behind me, a lady stood up and raised her hand. Pastor Bill responded and said, "The Holy Spirit touch you as He showed me." That very second, the power of God blasted her to the floor, and the tumor instantly dissolved! She stood up testifying that it was gone! Upon witnessing this, my jaw dropped and I was speechless. How did he know she was here? How did he know there was a tumor by her stomach? How did the power of God immediately dissolve the tumor?

The moment I saw this, my spirit began to cry out within me. I believed God could do anything, but witnessing it before my very eyes was a whole different matter. I knew that God shows no partiality (Romans 2:11) and if He would give this gift to Pastor Bill, He desires to give it to me, too.

As I sat there, my spirit was crying within me. Echoes resounded through the corridors of my soul, saying, "God... I must have this! I must have this! For the nations who do not know You, for India, I must have this anointing!" As tears began pouring from my eyes, I could no longer pay attention to the message. I was consumed with hunger and passion. I desperately needed what Pastor Bill Johnson had. I began to cry within myself so loud that I could not hear anything around me, "Oh God, I pray that Pastor Bill would lay his hands on me! Oh Father, let him lay his hands on me!"

I want you to know that my eyes were not focused on a man, nor was I trusting in a man for the anointing. Just the opposite. My eyes were locked on the Holy Spirit, and my hope was in Him alone. But, where was the Holy Spirit manifesting at that time? He was upon Pastor Bill. See, this is where many people fail to receive from God. Some people look to a man and walk away empty. Some people are too prideful and arrogant to have someone more anointed lay hands on them. Others say, "Well, if God wants me to have that anointing, He will just put it on me. I don't need to go anywhere to receive the anointing." Such leaders are too prideful and jealous, and that sin stops them from receiving. We cannot receive from God and reject His church at the same time. Often we receive from God through His church. God loves humility, and humility is most greatly revealed when we humble ourselves before others and seek help.

Toward the end of the sermon, Pastor Bill said, "If anyone needs prayer, come now to the front." I felt like a 100-yard sprinter in the Olympics. Though I was seated furthest back, I ran to the front and reached before anyone else. I fell on my knees, closed my eyes, and began to weep and cry out to God. Though my eyes were closed, I could feel Pastor Bill's hand upon my head. At that very moment, a fire flooded my being; my body began to shaking immensely, I instantly broke out in a sweat as I felt like my body was on fire. Shaking, I fell backwards on the ground as power pulsated through my body. Tears were flowing as I felt engulfed by a power that was uncontrollable and so much greater than anything I could ever imagine. As the power flowed inside of me, I began to see visions, and the Lord spoke to me about His great love and compassion for the nations of the earth.

I don't remember how much time passed while I was laying on the floor, but I knew that I knew my life was changed and the anointing in my life increased to a whole new level. After that experience, the Lord began to use me in the same way He used Pastor Bill, by giving me words of knowledge and, as a result, the blind are now seeing, the deaf are hearing, and tumors have instantly dissolved.

I am so thankful and grateful for amazing men of God, like Pastor Bill Johnson, who model for us what is possible in God's kingdom, but I am even more thankful for the Holy Spirit—that He would use a vessel such as me, so unworthy of His goodness.

Remember that God is pleased with faith, and the hungry get fed. The baptism of the Holy Spirit is within the reach of your hungry heart. Look to Him and receive!

Dismissing Irrational Fears

Before knowing the truth about the baptism of the Holy Spirit, I was told many negative things that set my thoughts against the baptism. I was told to "beware" of people who spoke in tongues, those people who unknowingly are blaspheming God in another language. A famous radio preacher spoke daily against the moves of the Spirit, calling it an "esoteric experience" rooted in "psychological hallucinations" and "demonic activity." I was warned to be on the defense against such teachings, that opening up your spirit to such could cause you to be demonized and deceived.

Are such concerns logical? Sure. Are such concerns Biblical? No. Jesus directly answers such absurd fears, and the Bible promises protection against such things. Read the following scripture.

> Which of you fathers, if your son asks for bread, will give him a stone? Or if he asks for a fish, he won't give him a snake instead of a fish, will he? Or if he asks for an egg, he won't give him a scorpion, will he? If you then, being evil, know how to give good gifts to your children, how much more will your heavenly Father give the Holy Spirit to those who ask him?
>
> — Luke 11:11–13

The context of this Scripture is prayer—asking and seeking God for blessings and the greatest blessing of all, the Holy Spirit. Jesus, comparing evil men to God, teaches how absurd it is to even think that God will give you something evil when you are asking for something good. It is important to note that scorpions and snakes represent the demonic (Luke 10:19). Jesus is directly teaching that it is impossible to receive a demon when you are asking for the Holy Spirit from God! Remember, every good and perfect gift comes from above (James 1:17), from your loving Father who longs for you to know and receive His Spirit!

6

Spiritual Gifts
Part I

Miraculous Healing through a Word of Knowledge

I was at my home church in Kansas City on a recent Sunday in morning prayer prior to the service. I was excited about the message of faith I was about to preach, but I knew that without the presence of the Holy Spirit my sermon would be, at best, accepted as inspirational, but lacking power to change anyone's life. While in prayer, fellowshipping with the Holy Spirit, I saw a vision. I saw what appeared to be the stomach and intestines visible in a person's body, as if the skin and abdominal layer were removed. It appeared to me as a cartoon sketch rather than a real life image. Though I was understanding what I was seeing, I didn't know what God was trying to convey to me. So I said, "Lord, I don't understand. Explain it to me." I waited a moment and then saw a hand appear with a long, sharp knife. The hand then began to stab the stomach and intestines. It was very strange, and I was more perplexed afterwards. I asked the Holy Spirit again, "Holy Spirit, I still don't understand. What are You trying to show me?" Then, I heard the voice of the Spirit, saying, "There will be a woman in this church service who has a stomach intestinal disease, and she feels pain after she eats as if someone is stabbing her." I immediately noted what the Spirit spoke.

Toward the end of the sermon, I said to the crowd of about 400 people, "There is a woman here who has an intestinal disease that causes extreme pain, as if someone is stabbing you with a sharp knife. The Lord Jesus heals you now!" Due to a lack of time, I didn't seek to have her stand up or come forward.

About two weeks later, after arriving in India I received this email:

Dear Robert,

It's hard to write to someone and tell them how much they have changed your life when you never even really met them, but here I go. On August 22nd you came to The Rock and you talked about how God has given you the power to heal. Throughout your speech, I was amazed. I have been sick for the last year and a half and have seen so many doctors and still, to this day, have not found out what was wrong with me. A friend of mine has been telling me I need to get healed at church and I know that God does give people the power to heal, but I never understood how he could choose who he gave those powers to, so it was hard for me to believe it. At the end, you started calling people out, and when you got to my section, you said you saw someone who had major stomach problems and whenever they ate they got sick. That has been my life for the last year and a half and it has kept me from doing so many things. Every Friday I would spend the day going from doctor appointment to doctor appointment and from test to test, but no one had found anything. I don't know why I started getting sick but I do know that God healed me through you... I always wondered what life would be like if I were healthy again and I am healthy again... Thank you.

Sandy

Let's now examine what happened. I was fellowshipping with the Holy Spirit, and while focusing on His presence, He showed me a vision. The vision lasted only a few seconds. Usually, the revelation I receive comes very fast, stays just for a moment, and then disappears. Therefore, I always need to be aware and ready that He might be speaking to me. Also, the Holy Spirit will often use strange or odd visions to speak to me. When in doubt in my natural mind, I usually accept strange visions as from the Lord, mainly because I could not have thought of them myself. As I saw the vision and didn't understand what I was seeing, I immediately asked the Holy Spirit for understanding. Listen to me carefully: Do not try to understand the vision or word by your own wisdom or discernment! It is the Holy Spirit's responsibility to show us, and it is also His responsibility to explain what He is showing. The Holy Spirit gave me limited revelation: woman, stomach intestinal disease, and stabbing pain after eating. Note that I didn't know her age, name, or anything else. He gives us what we need to know to partner with Him. Excessive revelation tends to glorify man instead of God. What I then did was very simple. I shared with the crowd what I saw and in faith said, "Jesus Christ heals you." Then, an undiagnosable, chronic disease that lasted for 1.5 years instantly vanished. We do so very little, and He does so very much!

THE PURPOSE OF THE GIFTS

In this chapter, I want to teach you about the gifts of the Spirit, what they are, and how they operate. But first, we will examine their purpose.

> But to each one is given the manifestation of the Spirit for the profit of all.
>
> — 1 Corinthians 12:7

> Even Jesus of Nazareth, how God anointed Him with the Holy Spirit and with power, who went about doing good and healing all who were oppressed by the devil, for God was with him... He who sins is of the devil, for the devil has been sinning from the beginning. To this end, the Son of God was revealed: that He might destroy the works of the devil.
>
> — Acts 10:38 & 1 John 3:8

But he who prophesies speaks to men for their edification, exhortation, and consolation.

— 1 Corinthians 14:3

The purpose of the gifts of the Spirit is for the profit of all. When I first started walking in healing miracle power, I heard the Lord say to me, "I did not anoint you for your sake, but for the sake of others." I quickly learned that it was never about me, but all about His great love for others. The second purpose of the gifts is to destroy the works of the devil. The devil has taken many captive, both believers and unbelievers, and it is through these gifts that his grip and power is destroyed. Thirdly, the gifts are given to edify, encourage, and comfort. The gifts of the Spirit will always produce these results. If not, then you should question if it is the Holy Spirit's power or that of a devil.

In 1 Corinthians 12:4–11, we see nine gifts of the Spirit listed. I want to categorize these gifts so that we can understand them better. Below are the categories:

1. Gifts of Revelation
2. Speaking Gifts
3. Gifts of Power

In this chapter, I want to exclusively focus on the gifts of revelation. The other gifts will be discussed in Chapter 7.

Note: While discussing revelation gifts, I will refer to the Greek word *rhema* several times. In the Greek, there are two words for the word "word". One is *logos*, which refers to the written Bible we now read. The other is *rhema*, which refers to the present spoken word from God that we hear directly from Him.

Gifts of Revelation

Words of Wisdom

Word of wisdom: Divine wisdom for a specific situation, in which knowledge needs to be applied, a decision needs to be made, or a response needs to be given, so that the will of God may be fulfilled.

Wisdom is the ability to apply knowledge at the right time, in the right situation. Some people are very knowledgeable but are still fools because they are unable to apply the knowledge they have. The Bible declares that Jesus is our shepherd, and we are His sheep. When the Bible calls us "sheep," this is not an encouragement. Sheep are very stupid animals, illustrating our great need for a wise shepherd.

Jesus said that in His place He would send another Helper. Jesus is now in heaven, and our current shepherd on earth is the Holy Spirit (John 16:13). A word of wisdom is a *rhema* word from the Holy Spirit to you, instructing you in that specific situation. Below is an example from the life of Jesus.

> They asked him, "Teacher, we know that you say and teach what is right, and aren't partial to anyone, but truly teach the way of God. Is it lawful for us to pay taxes to Caesar, or not?" But he perceived their craftiness, and said to them, "Why do you test me? Show me a denarius. Whose image and inscription are on it?" They answered, "Caesar's." He said to them, "Then give to Caesar the things that are Caesar's, and to God the things that are God's."
>
> — Luke 20:21–25

The Lord has given me the privilege to travel to many places and minister in the power of the Kingdom. But, I have found that not every pastor, leader, and minister is excited about the healing ministry. Many in the church are spiritually crippled by disappointment that has brought bitterness to their hearts. For some, a loved one died of cancer. Others have broken marriages, or a prodigal child. When we talk about the impossible becoming possible, many such people respond with arguments and anger. In those situations when I felt "cornered" by other leaders who were arguing with me about God's goodness, I often receive words of wisdom, knowing what to say and what not to say (Proverbs 15:1). Words that I never thought of would come out of my mouth, winning my accusers and softening their hearts to believe again.

An Old Testament example of this gift is found in 1 Kings 3:16–28. Anytime the Spirit instructs you, or someone through you, what to do in a situation or how to do it, that is a word of wisdom.

Words of Knowledge

Word of knowledge: Divine knowledge for a specific situation about a person, place, or event. This knowledge is either about the past, present, or both, but never about the future. This knowledge is a guide for prayer, evangelism, healing, deliverance, or a miracle.

There are many such examples of this gift in scripture (John 4:16–19, Matthew 16:13–17). In the story of Jesus healing the paralytic man, we read below...

> But there were some of the scribes sitting there and reasoning in their hearts, "Why does this man speak blasphemies like that? Who can forgive sins but God alone?" Immediately Jesus, perceiving in his spirit that they so reasoned within themselves, said to them, "Why do you reason these things in your hearts?"
>
> — Mark 2:6–8

Some people just think that Jesus knew everything because He was the Son of God. We found that common belief to be false in Chapter 3. Jesus, in that moment, received a word of knowledge and knew by the Holy Spirit what they were thinking.

Most of my experiences with words of knowledge are related to healing, deliverance, and miracles. A word of knowledge is the *rhema* word of the Holy Spirit for that moment.

I was invited to Maharashtra for a three-day healing meeting. On the evening of the second day, before speaking, I saw a vision. In the vision, I saw a stomach and intestines, and wrapped around them was a green snake. A snake is very clear symbol of the demonic in Scripture (Luke 10:19). I then immediately heard the Holy Spirit's voice, "There is a man in this meeting who cannot digest food because a demon is afflicting him." After preaching, I called out the word like this, "The man here who has a stomach problem and is not able to digest food, stand up." In a crowd of about 2,000 people, a man in the back stood up. I looked at him and said, "As the Lord showed me, so be it unto you. In Jesus's name, afflicting devil, come out and leave him!" I then had him sit down.

The third night of the meeting, this man came up on stage when we were sharing testimonies. He was an unbeliever. He said he was unable to eat anything for many days, and he heard about the healings that were happening here, so he came. He testified that ever since he stood up, after I gave the word, he was instantly and completely healed. Not knowing it was God who healed him, he tried to prostrate himself before me in honor. I stopped him and explained that Jesus alone healed him.

God always wants to heal, deliver, and perform miracles. I do not encourage people to look for or wait for a word of knowledge for their needs, but rather to believe God now. So, why is a word of knowledge special? A word of knowledge declares that there is special grace at that moment for that condition or need, and when acted upon, God moves powerfully.

A word of knowledge declares that there is special grace at that moment for that condition or need, and when acted upon, God moves powerfully.

Prophecy

Prophecy: This gift has two different functions. (1) Knowledge related to the will of God about the future of a specific person, place or situation. This knowledge of the future can be affected by faith, decisions, and actions. Or (2) God's *rhema* word released through speaking that strengthens, builds up, and brings peace to others. Examples in Scripture are Matthew 16:21, Acts 13:1–3, 20:22–23, and 21:10–11.

To understand prophecy, there needs to be much explaining, for many understand it as fate, meaning that it will always come to pass. Except for a few special prophecies, such as Jesus's return, the salvation of Israel, the final judgment, etc., prophecy is not fate but an invitation to the will of God. Prophecy is God sharing His heart with you about His wonderful will for your life. Prophecies can be resisted and thwarted by our unbelief and ungodly actions.

Once I was in Unnao, Uttar Pradesh, at a church service. Afterwards, I was praying for many sick. A lady came up to me who was barren and had tried for eight years to have a child. After praying for her, I said, "You will immediately become pregnant, and within this year you will have a child." I didn't think before I spoke. It just came out of my mouth! After saying it, I was a little frightened, thinking, "What if it doesn't come to pass?" I returned to Unnao and found out that she had immediately become pregnant and that same year she bore a son!

This was a word of prophecy, revealing God's will for her future. But you need to understand that she acted in faith upon hearing that word. She went home and became intimate with her husband. She could have chosen to disbelieve and to not have sexual relations with her husband for that year. If she did such, she would not have born a child. Prophecy is an invitation to the will and power of God.

Also, prophecy is not always about the future. Most prophecies that I have given and heard are the message of God's heart to someone, and it has nothing to do with the future.

But he who prophesies speaks to men for their edification, exhortation, and consolation.

— 1 Corinthians 14:3

For example, while ministering to others, I receive words of prophecy, such as, "The Father wants to tell you that He loves you deeply, He has been thinking about you, and you are not to worry for He is faithfully with you," or, "You are precious in His sight. You are His cherished daughter, and He values you so much."

In my experience, about 90% of prophecies are a message from God's heart that comforts, encourages, and strengthens the hearer. About 10% are words relating to the future.

Basically, prophecy is a message from God's heart to you and an invitation to know and live in His will. The difference between a word of knowledge and prophecy is this: Words of knowledge are revelation *about* a person, but words of prophecy are a message *from* God's heart *to* a person.

Discerning of Spirits

Discerning of Spirits: The spiritual capacity given in a specific situation for the purpose of identifying and responding to God, angels, or demons in the spiritual realm. Examples in scripture are Luke 13:10–16, Acts 13:8–12 and 2 Kings 6:8–18.

It is my conviction that God, His angels, and demons are present at most places and situations, but we are usually unaware of it. Often when I am preaching to a crowd of hundreds or thousands, there are angels present, as well as demons upon and inside of many people who are sick and afflicted. When we are able, for a moment, to see an angel or demon, we get excited and think, "I see one!" We might see one, but trust me, there are many that we don't see.

The gift of discerning of spirits is the grace of the Holy Spirit upon us for a short period of time to see what is happening in the spirit realm. We won't see all the demons and their work, but only a specific few whose works we are to confront and destroy at that moment.

Let me give you some examples. I was in Redding, California, at a Bethel Church leaders conference. Toward the end of one of the sessions, we were encouraged to pray for ourselves and others for spiritual increase. While in prayer, I felt a strong, heavy presence coming toward the front of my body. The closer the presence came to me, the heavier the presence felt. When it felt to be about five or six feet from me, suddenly electricity shot out toward me and hit me. My entire body convulsed, and I fell to the floor, shaking. While lying down, I looked up in front of me and saw an angel. It was wearing a white dress down to its knees. Its face was so radiant that I could not distinguish the eyes, nose, and other facial features from the bright light. The wings were tucked behind, and on its arms and legs there was no hair at all. His skin appeared very smooth.

Then the angel spoke to me, but not with words from the mouth, but rather through telepathy. Its thoughts were projected from his mind into mine, saying, "I am a miracle angel who the Lord has sent to you. You will not always see me, but know that I am with you." As fast as you can blink your eyes, it was gone. No one else in the room saw it but me. Why was I the only one to see and hear this angel? Because only I was given the gift of discerning of spirits for that specific moment.

After this powerful encounter, I went to Maharashtra, India, to attend a healing meeting. I was invited to speak one night to a crowd of about 3,000 people. After preaching, I began to pray for the sick, and during that time, I saw angels in the crowd. Over to the side, I saw a man who appeared very sick, having his hands raised during the mass prayer. A moment later, I looked over again, and he was laying on the ground, unconscious.

After prayer, we invited those who were healed and delivered to come up and testify. That same man came up and began to share that he felt someone touch him and how electricity flowed into his body and he fell down (just like I did!). When he got up, he was healed of all body pain. He tested his body, and there was not a trace of any disease left in him! He said he suffered from several chronic illnesses, but all their symptoms disappeared!

On another occasion, I was praying for a woman who was suffering from depression and many emotional problems. Upon inviting the Holy Spirit's presence, I immediately saw a vision. My sight in the vision was like a camera view. I was in an enclosed room, and on the other side was a door that was shut. As I approached the door, my sight went toward the keyhole on the door and went through the keyhole. I entered into another room that looked similar to the first, with a door on the other side. My sight went toward that door, and through that door's keyhole. This happened a total of four times. As I was in the fourth room and went through the fourth keyhole, I entered another room that had a young girl sleeping on a bed. I had a sense that the girl was about four years of age. Then I saw an evil spirit climb up the bed and stand over her. The girl, in her sleep, started to panic. She was moaning and moving around. The spirit entered her, and the girl sat up in bed, screaming and crying.

After seeing this, I looked at her and said, "From the age of four, you started to have horrible nightmares and panic attacks in the night." She confirmed it and said, "Yes, but how did you know?" I then commanded, "The spirit of fear from the fourth generation, come out of her now!" The spirit immediately manifested and left.

The vision I saw lasted a few seconds, 10 at most. I had an impression that explained what I was seeing. There were four empty rooms, meaning that from four generations, this spirit had passed down. Each key hole symbolizes authority, meaning each generation gave authority to this spirit to abide and remain. This was a very specific discerning of spirits gift. At other times, it is not as detailed but is just as effective.

When we are operating in this gift, we are allowed to speak, hear, identify, recognize, and affect the spirit realm in a special way.

When we are operating in this gift, we are allowed to speak, hear, identify, recognize, and affect the spirit realm in a special way. This gift is highly effective at destroying demonic powers and casting out evil spirits, as well as partnering with angels.

I will give you one more example of how this works. I was in Varanasi, teaching at a conference about God's love. It was not a healing or deliverance meeting. People came to learn about our Heavenly Father and His great love for the nations. At the very end of the conference, many people were coming up to receive prayer for mostly spiritual needs. I saw a man in the prayer line, waiting, who I had met two years before. But he looked very, very ill. From a distance I could see that both of his eyes were very yellow, and he looked extremely frail and weak.

When it was his turn for prayer, I asked him what was wrong. He explained that he was suffering from jaundice for 3–4 months. His liver was in pain, and he had lost much weight. He went to several doctors and was taking medicine, but he found no relief. His condition looked so bad that if he didn't find a cure or a miracle, he would die.

Before praying for him, I invited the Holy Spirit, "Holy Spirit, my Beloved, come upon me, and be with me. I give You the pre-eminence at this time." I then laid my hand on top of his liver. Immediately, a flow of power surged from my shoulder, through my arm and hand, and into his body. The flow of power was so intense that I could not even speak to pray. I just stood there, with my hand on him, shaking. He was shaking too, but not to the degree I was. After about one or two minutes, the flow of power stopped. I asked him, "How do you feel now?" He was astonished at the power he felt, and he replied that all the pain and weakness in his body was gone. He felt completely healed.

I smiled and said, "You can go now." As he turned and started to walk away, I heard the voice of the Spirit say, "Do not let him go! The war is not yet over. Cast a spirit of death out of him." I yelled out, "Hey! Come back here! I need to pray some more for you!" He came back, and I told him to look into my eyes. I stared in his eyes, commanding, "You spirit of death! I command you to leave him now and come out!" The moment I spoke this, he convulsed and shook for just a moment. I asked him what he felt. He replied that from his abdomen area he felt an evil presence come out of him. Since I didn't receive any more guidance, I let him go. The next day at the Varanasi train station, it happened that we suddenly met, and he was telling everyone how God healed him, how his strength and health were restored, and within 24 hours his eyes had turned white!

In that situation, I was given the gift of discerning of spirits to recognize and command that spirit to leave. When this gift is operating, the spirit is immediately evicted without a fight, because the grace and power of the Holy Spirit is present.

Interpretation of Tongues

Interpretation of tongues: The special ability in a specific situation to understand an unknown language.

I put this gift under "revelation gifts" instead of "speaking gifts" because of the need to clarify and teach on how we actually interpret what we are hearing. Like all revelation gifts, the way the interpretation comes to us is by spiritual revelation.

> What is it then, brothers? When you come together, each one of you has a psalm, has a teaching, has a revelation, has another language, has an interpretation. Let all things be done to build each other up. If any man speaks in another language, let it be two, or at the most three, and in turn; and let one interpret.
>
> — 1 Corinthians 14:26–27

This gift is used in conjunction with the gift of speaking in tongues. When someone speaks in an unknown language or a heavenly language, the individual speaking, or another person present, will often receive the interpretation. The interpretation can come in various forms and ways, about which I will be sharing next. I have found that interpretation of tongues is very similar to prophecy, in that it is a message from God's heart to a person or a group of people. The difference between interpretation of tongues and prophecy is how it is delivered. For interpretation, a tongue will proceed with the interpretation following. This tongue is like a "trumpet sound" grabbing the attention of the hearer, preparing them for what God is about to say.

The Various Forms of Revelation Gifts

We just defined the five revelation gifts so that we can identify them and their purposes. Now we are going to learn how we receive these gifts. I will be teaching the most common ways they are received. This list is not complete, but rather, it explains the major ways the average person receives these gifts. The ways are visions, dreams, hearing a voice, impressions, and emotional or physical feelings. We must understand that any of the revelation gifts, be it words of wisdom, discerning of spirits, or interpretation of tongues, can come by any of these ways. Prophecy might come in a vision at one time, but in another situation, it might come as an impression. If we know how the Holy Spirit commonly speaks to people, then we can be more attentive to His voice.

Visions	There are two types of visions; open and closed. Open visions are seen with the physical eyes. Closed visions are seen with the eyes of the heart or spirit; very similar to ones imagination. By far the more common of the two are closed visions. A vision is a picture or video revealed by the Holy Spirit. While seeing a vision there is often a need for interpretation.
Dreams	Very similar to a vision but seen while asleep.

A Voice	There are two types of voices that are heard; an audible voice heard with the physical ear and an inner voice heard with the spiritual ear.
Impressions	A sudden knowing that comes without seeing a vision or hearing a voice.
Feelings	A sudden feeling, whether emotional or physical, that gives you insight and understanding.

Now, let's look at several examples in Scripture:

> I was in the city of Joppa praying, and in a trance I saw a vision: a certain container descending, like it was a great sheet let down from heaven by four corners. It came as far as me. When I had looked intently at it, I considered, and saw the four-footed animals of the earth, wild animals, creeping things, and birds of the sky. I also heard a voice saying to me, "Rise, Peter, kill and eat!" But I said, "Not so, Lord, for nothing unholy or unclean has ever entered into my mouth." But a voice answered me the second time out of heaven, "What God has cleansed, don't you call unclean." This was done three times, and all were drawn up again into heaven.
>
> — Acts 11:5–10

In examining this event, we can see that Peter saw a vision, but we are not sure if he saw it with his physical eyes or spiritual eyes. While seeing the vision, he also heard the voice of the Spirit speaking to him. Peter received a word of prophecy through a vision and hearing a voice. This was a word of prophecy because God was sharing a personal message with Peter. This message instructed Peter to go to the Gentiles and minister to them.

When they had gone through the region of Phrygia and Galatia, they were forbidden by the Holy Spirit to speak the word in Asia. When they had come opposite Mysia, they tried to go into Bithynia, but the Spirit didn't allow them. Passing by Mysia, they came down to Troas. A vision appeared to Paul in the night. There was a man of Macedonia standing, begging him, and saying, "Come over into Macedonia and help us." When he had seen the vision, immediately we sought to go out to Macedonia, concluding that the Lord had called us to preach the Good News to them.

— Acts 16:6–10

Because of a lack of explanation from Scripture, we are unsure how the Holy Spirit forbid them. Later, Paul received a word of prophecy through seeing a vision and hearing a voice. This word of prophecy was a message that directed and instructed Paul where to go and what to do.

At Lystra, a certain man sat, impotent in his feet, a cripple from his mother's womb, who never had walked. He was listening to Paul speaking, who, fastening eyes on him and seeing that he had faith to be made whole, said with a loud voice, "Stand upright on your feet!" He leaped up and walked.

— Acts 14:8–10

Paul saw the invisible faith of the crippled man. How did he see it? He saw it through a vision. Paul saw in the spirit realm the man's faith. This revelation was a word of knowledge—knowledge about that man's spiritual capacity to receive the healing power of God at that moment. Like many words of knowledge, Paul spoke out what he saw and said, "Stand up!" and immediately, the miraculous healing took place.

> But there were some of the scribes sitting there and reasoning in their hearts, "Why does this man speak blasphemies like that? Who can forgive sins but God alone?" Immediately Jesus, perceiving in his spirit that they so reasoned within themselves, said to them, "Why do you reason these things in your hearts?"
>
> — Mark 2:6–8

Jesus, through a word of knowledge that came by an impression, understood what those people were thinking. Jesus did not see a vision, nor did He hear a voice. Suddenly, His spirit perceived and understood something that was impossible to know without revelation. This is what an impression is.

> He was teaching in one of the synagogues on the Sabbath day. Behold, there was a woman who had a spirit of infirmity eighteen years, and she was bent over, and could in no way straighten herself up. When Jesus saw her, he called her and said to her, "Woman, you are freed from your infirmity." He laid his hands on her, and immediately she stood up straight and glorified God... Therefore, the Lord answered him... "Ought not this woman, being a daughter of Abraham, whom Satan had bound eighteen long years, be freed from this bondage on the Sabbath day?"
>
> — Luke 13:10–16

We are unsure how Jesus was able to perceive the demon afflicting this woman, such as a vision or impression, but we are certain that He was operating in the gift of discerning of spirits. Through this gift, Jesus was able to identify the source of the problem, a demon, and respond to it in an effective manner.

I was conducting a seminar on the gifts of the Holy Spirit to about 100 leaders in 2009. After teaching on words of knowledge, I demonstrated it by giving several words that resulted in instantaneous healings. Then, I invited ten people to come and receive a word of knowledge for others in the training. They were very timid, because prior to this event, they had never received a word of knowledge, nor had they received any prior training. I laid my hands upon each of them, imparting the gift by faith. I then asked them to remain silent and focus on the Holy Spirit.

One man said he suddenly felt pain in his forehead and in his chest. He knew that it was not his pain, because prior to this event, he had never suffered from pain in those areas. I then asked the crowd if anyone had pain in those areas. A woman stood up and said, "That is me. I have head pain in my forehead and in my chest." I had him pray for her. As he prayed for the pain in her forehead, her pain disappeared, and the pain he was feeling also disappeared. But the pain in the chest remained. He then prayed for the chest pain to leave her, and as it left her, so did the pain in his chest. She was immediately healed. This is an example of how emotional or physical feelings can be indications of the Holy Spirit's leading and guidance in our lives, so that we can effectively minister to others.

When we understand the purpose of the gifts and how they come, we are much more prepared to receive and partner with the Holy Spirit. If I feel I am receiving a word of knowledge, I immediately understand what God wants to do at that very moment, which increases and strengthens my faith. God only desires simple faith and obedience from us. When we do our part, then He does great and amazing miracles! Earnestly desire the gifts (1 Corinthians 14:1), but even more so desire the gift Giver and cherish Him!

> *When we understand the purpose of the gifts and how they come, we are much more prepared to receive and partner with the Holy Spirit.*

7

Spiritual Gifts
Part II

SPEAKING GIFT

In this chapter we are going to define and understand the other two kinds of gifts: speaking gifts and gifts of power.

Various Tongues – The divine enabling to speak in an unknown language.

While Peter was still speaking these words, the Holy Spirit fell on all those who heard the word. They of the circumcision who believed were amazed, as many as came with Peter, because the gift of the Holy Spirit was also poured out on the Gentiles. For they heard them speaking in other languages and magnifying God.

— Acts 10:44–46

When Paul had laid his hands on them, the Holy Spirit came on them, and they spoke with other languages and prophesied.

— Acts 19:6

There are two different ways the gift of tongues operates. One is for personal prayer, and the other is a message for others used in conjunction with the gift of interpretation of tongues.

"Personal Prayer" Tongues

Just as we are able to pray and worship God in different known languages, such as Hindi, English, Urdu, Spanish etc., so this gift gives us the ability to pray and worship in an unknown language. Whenever anyone is in prayer or worship to the Lord, they are speaking directly to Him in whatever language they understand. When anyone prays or worships in tongues, their words are directly to the Lord, not according to a language they mentally understand, but rather from the depths of their spirit. Praying and worshiping in tongues is applicable in any setting or situation where normal prayer and worship is applicable. The Bible encourages us to pray in a known language with our mental understanding, but also to pray from the spirit in tongues.

> For he who speaks in another language speaks not to men, but to God, for no one understands; but in the Spirit, he speaks mysteries.
>
> — 1 Corinthians 14:2

> What is it then? I will pray with the spirit, and I will pray with the understanding also. I will sing with the spirit, and I will sing with the understanding also.
>
> — 1 Corinthians 14:15

	FOUR BENEFITS OF PRAYING IN TONGUES
1.	Strengthening the spirit man (1 Corinthians 14:4)
2.	Increasing in faith (Jude 20)
3.	Praying according to the will of God by the leading of the Holy Spirit
4.	Becoming more sensitive to the spirit realm and the presence of God

"Message" Tongues

The purpose of this type of tongue is not for praying or worshiping in an unknown language, nor is it directed to the Lord, but rather it is a message directed to a person or a group of people. For the message to be revealed through this type of tongue, the gift of interpretation of tongues is absolutely necessary. This type of tongue is only applicable when God wants to speak a message to a person or group of people. After the tongue is given, the Holy Spirit will give the gift of interpretation of tongues to either the one speaking or to another in the meeting. The interpretation comes for the purpose of guiding, strengthening, comforting, and edifying. If there is no interpretation for this type of tongue, the Apostle Paul instructs the one speaking in tongues to be silent. This type of tongue used with the gift of interpretation is very similar to the gift of prophecy in that it is a message from God's heart to a person or a group of people.

> I thank my God, I speak with other languages more than you all. However, in the assembly I would rather speak five words with my understanding, that I might instruct others also, than ten thousand words in another language.
>
> — 1 Corinthians 14:18–19

> If any man speaks in another language, let it be two, or at the most three, and in turn; and let one interpret. But if there is no interpreter, let him keep silent in the assembly, and let him speak to himself, and to God.
>
> — 1 Corinthians 14:27–28

POWER GIFTS

The last group of gifts we are going to learn about are the power gifts. These power gifts are: faith, miracles, and healing. These gifts are graces released to the church for specific occasions, as the Holy Spirit wills (1 Corinthians 12:11). These gifts are according to the *rhema* voice of the Spirit. Often, gifts of revelation precede the gifts of power, giving us guidance and insight, both working together effectively.

There is a big distinction between these gifts and obeying God's Word with common faith. At any time, in any situation, I can obey God's *logos*, written Word, in faith and expect results, such as healing and miracles. This is not a manifestation of a power gift. he differences between these gifts and common faith that produces healing and miracles:

1. The power gifts are directed by the *rhema* voice of the Spirit, whereas common faith comes by the *logos* written Word.

2. The power gifts manifest as the Spirit wills, whereas common faith produces results as we respond in a situation according to what the Bible says.

3. The power gifts are for specific situations, whereas common faith can be applied anywhere, in any situation, and at any time.

For example, not every healing that happens is due to the gifts of healing. Jesus declared that they will lay hands on the sick and they will recover (Mark 16:18). This healing often happens because of simple faith, trust, and obedience to the word of God, and not due to the gifts of healing. Understanding this distinction is very important in operating in these gifts. These power gifts are graces of the Spirit that go beyond the reach of our normal faith, trust, and obedience to God's Word.

Gift of Faith

> *Gift of Faith –* An impartation of divine faith in which there is no doubt or unbelief. This impartation of faith is for a specific situation, in which the person's normal faith is insufficient for the miracle needed.

This gift of faith is separate from a believer's normal faith and only lasts for a specific need. Normal faith comes by knowing God's word and voice and is in a process of growth and maturity (Romans 10:17, Matthew 14:22–31). But the gift of faith is not so. It is an impartation of God's perfect and mature faith.

People who operate in this gift have testified that they have experienced a heightened level of faith. A strong boldness overcomes them, and what they are believing for always comes to pass. When the gift lifts, their faith returns to normal. This gift is often used for miraculous healings, financial provisions, or any situation that seems impossible.

> Jesus answered them, "Have faith in God. For most certainly I tell you, whoever may tell this mountain, "Be taken up and cast into the sea," and doesn't doubt in his heart, but believes that what he says is happening; he shall have whatever he says.
>
> — Mark 11:22–23

Most Bible translations have verse 22 translated incorrectly. According to the Greek, the proper translation should be, "Have the God kind of faith" or "Have the faith of God." Though we can apply this Scripture to our daily lives with our normal faith, this scripture is speaking specifically of the gift of faith. The gift of faith is an impartation of God's perfect faith. When we are walking in God's faith, there is no doubt, and whatever we speak and declare will always come to pass. The gift of faith gives absolute assurance that what someone is believing for will come to pass.

I want to share Pastor Ankit Sajwan's testimony as a practical example of this gift. There was a young couple in his church, who he was mentoring. One day, Ankit received a call from the lady, and she was weeping loudly. Ankit asked her what was wrong. She replied that her fiancé had been in pain for the past few days, so they decided to consult a doctor. Upon meeting the doctor, they learned that he had a bad case of appendicitis. The doctors warned them that the appendix could burst at any moment and told them immediate surgery was required. While crying, she told Ankit that they didn't have money for the surgery.

Great faith rose up in Ankit's heart, and he immediately proclaimed, "No surgical knife will touch his body! Don't go for the surgery. I am coming right now to pray for him."

Ankit clearly shared that this was not his usual faith, because the situation was very dire and every moment that delayed the surgery could lead to life-threatening complications. "But this faith was very different," Ankit said. "It felt like whatever I had decreed would come to pass, and there was no doubt concerning it."

Ankit took some of the leaders of his church and went to the hospital right away. They prayed for him according to James 5:14, pouring oil on his head. After prayer, his pain disappeared, and he was completely healed without surgery or any medicines.

Working of Miracles

> *Working of Miracles* – An impartation of divine power in a specific situation for the purpose of performing a miracle.

Some examples are: Matthew 14:22–32, John 2:1–11, 6:1–14 and 2 Kings 6:1–6.

The workings of miracles function when we act or speak according to the leading of the Holy Spirit.

While ministering once in Manmad, Maharashtra, a lady attended our healing meeting who had broken her arm and wrist two years previously. The doctors performed surgery and inserted a metal rod into her arm and wrist. Since that surgery, she was unable to move her wrist in certain positions.

After receiving prayer, she noticed something very strange. Her wrist became completely movable and flexible in every direction! She stated that this could not be possible, because there was a metal rod in her arm and wrist! Well, the Holy Spirit dissolved either part of the rod or the entire rod, because her wrist was healed and now moving! This is not just a healing, but a miracle!

Gifts of Healing

Gifts of Healings – An impartation of divine healing power in a specific situation for the healing of various and specific diseases; physical, emotional and/or mental.

This is the only gift that is plural in the Greek. There are "gifts" of "healings." Meaning, in this category are different kinds of healings for different kinds of afflictions.

I have noticed in various meetings that the Holy Spirit will highlight a specific disease or affliction. For example, it might be joint pain and arthritis, or it might be back problems or deafness. Sometimes it is emotional, such as fear and anxiety. This leading toward a specific disease might come through words of knowledge. As we pray about those specific illnesses, we see incredible breakthrough. Sometimes we do not have a specific leading before the meeting, but as people are coming up to share their testimonies, we see that many people with a specific problem are healed, such as breathing problems or asthma. When we feel that this gift is being manifested, we will often be more aggressive toward that type of disease or demonic affliction, inviting everyone in the meeting or area to immediately receive prayer.

Passionately Desiring Gifts through Submission to His Will

Apostle Paul encourages the church to earnestly desire the gifts of the Spirit. We are to study them, share testimonies about them, pray for them, and seek them. Our spirit man should be in a state of hunger and desire for the gifts. Why? Because God only satisfies the hungry!

> Blessed are those who hunger and thirst after righteousness, for they shall be filled.
>
> — Matthew 5:6

We must understand two very important truths as we seek to operate in the gifts. First, we should never desire the gifts more than the gift Giver. Whenever our passion for the gifts is greater than our passion for the Holy Spirit, then we get off track and follow down a path that leads to selfish ambitions and the glory of man. I seek to love and know Him and to make myself available to be used by Him. If I am in constant fellowship with Him, then the gifts of the Spirit will flow easily through me.

Second, the operations of the gifts are according to His desire and will, not according to our will or passion. We cannot choose what the Holy Spirit will do in a specific situation. We have to get direction from Him. He does not get direction from us!

> But the one and the same Spirit produces all of these, distributing to each one separately as he desires.
>
> — 1 Corinthians 12:11

Someone might think, "Why passionately desire the gifts if He chooses what He wants to do? What role does my passion have?" He will distribute the gifts as He desires at specific times and places, but usually He will only use the gifts through those people who are in fellowship with Him, who passionately desire the gifts and whose will is in submission to His.

Hear me clearly now, as you begin to operate in the gifts, you will come to discover that He wants to do more than we could ever think or imagine! He wants to speak more than most believers are prepared to hear. This is where our faith comes into the picture. If I believe that He might want to speak, then my faith is low. If I know that He always wants to speak and I am attentive and ready to hear, then my faith is high. *According to our faith, so let it be done to us!* (Matthew 8:13)

> *I have a strong confidence that God wants to heal people now. He wants to speak to people now. I don't need to convince or pressure Him to move, because I believe He wants to move more than I want Him to!*

I have a strong confidence that God wants to heal people now. He wants to speak to people now. I don't need to convince or pressure Him to move, because I believe He wants to move more than I want Him to! What I need to do is hear what He is speaking, and understand to whom He wants to speak, and who He wants to touch.

Does this mean if I do not have a leading from the Holy Spirit for a specific sick person in a meeting that God does not want to heal that person? Absolutely not! I can pray in faith for anyone at any time, regardless of whether or not I have any leading of the Spirit. God desires all to be healed, freed, forgiven, and blessed. But, following the leading of the Spirit proves more fruitful and is more effective. In most meetings, I follow the leading of the Spirit first, and when I do not have any more leadings, then I pray for others according to their needs. But, I give priority to the leading of the Spirit.

THE ANOINTING OF THE SPIRIT

Operating in the gifts of the Spirit comes by three practical ways:

1. The baptism of the Holy Spirit.

2. Learning from and ministering with someone who already walks in the Spirit.

3. Receiving an impartation from someone who is anointed by the Spirit of God.

I want to discuss the third practical way: an impartation from an anointed person. Read the Scriptures below.

> Don't neglect the gift that is in you, which was given to you by prophecy, with the laying on of the hands of the elders. Be diligent in these things. Give yourself wholly to them, that your progress may be revealed to all.
>
> — 1 Timothy 4:14–15

> For this cause, I remind you that you should stir up the gift of God which is in you through the laying on of my hands.
>
> — 2 Timothy 1:6

> For I long to see you, that I may impart to you some spiritual gift, to the end that you may be established.
>
> — Romans 1:11

These Scriptures clearly show that through the laying on of hands by an anointed person, such as the elders and the Apostle Paul, Timothy received a gift of the Spirit. This gift is not according to how Timothy wills, but according to how the Holy Spirit wills (1 Corinthians 12:11). But Timothy received a greater sensitivity to, and ability to operate in, that gift when the Holy Spirit willed.

For example, if I receive an impartation for the gift of prophecy, that impartation makes me sensitive to the gift of prophecy and gives me a greater capacity to walk in that gift.

Now understand this: I can't prophecy over whomever I want, whenever I want, all day long. But, I can operate in that gift to a greater degree as the Holy Spirit manifests it.

I have received many impartations over the years by leaders who were skilled in prophecy, words of knowledge and gifts of healings. As I received impartations, I noticed that my sensitivity to and ability to operate in these gifts increased.

Read the following Scriptures. In each verse, answer this question:

Through whom did the mighty works of the Spirit operate?

> Fear came on every soul, and many wonders and signs were done through the apostles.
>
> — Acts 2:43

> With great power, the apostles gave their testimony of the resurrection of the Lord Jesus. Great grace was on them all.
>
> — Acts 4:33

> By the hands of the apostles, many signs and wonders were done among the people.
>
> — Acts 5:12

From the time the Holy Spirit fell in Acts 2 all the way through Chapter 5, we see that miracles, signs, and wonders were performed only through the Apostles. But, a change takes place in Chapter 6.

Now in those days, when the number of the disciples was multiplying, a complaint arose from the Hellenists against the Hebrews, because their widows were neglected in the daily service. The twelve summoned the multitude of the disciples and said, "It is not appropriate for us to forsake the word of God and serve tables. Therefore, select from among you, brothers, seven men of good report, full of the Holy Spirit and of wisdom, whom we may appoint over this business. But we will continue steadfastly in prayer and in the ministry of the word." These words pleased the whole multitude. They chose Stephen, a man full of faith and of the Holy Spirit, Philip, Prochorus, Nicanor, Timon, Parmenas, and Nicolaus, a proselyte of Antioch, whom they set before the apostles. When they had prayed, they laid their hands on them. The word of God increased, and the number of the disciples multiplied in Jerusalem exceedingly. A great company of the priests were obedient to the faith. Stephen, full of faith and power, performed great wonders and signs among the people."

— Acts 6:1–8

In verse 6, we see that the Apostles laid hands upon Stephen and prayed over him. Then we see the immediate result in verse 8—that he performed great wonders and signs among the people. This is what an impartation is. The grace given to us is passed on to others, and the results are usually immediate. I will share several personal testimonies to establish this truth.

Several years ago, I was invited to teach during the morning and afternoon sessions at an All Maharashtra Pastors and Leaders Conference. During the evenings, I ministered at a healing meeting where several thousand people gathered, and the pastors and leaders in the conference attended the healing meeting as well. There was a pastor there named Santosh, who had been serving the Lord since 2004 in the northern part of Maharashtra that borders Madhya Pradesh. During his years of ministry, he saw very few healings and no miracles. In 2009, he came to the All Maharashtra Pastors and Leaders Conference and learned about miracles and how the Holy Spirit operates.

During the conference, I set one entire session aside to explain about impartation. After teaching, I prayed for the leaders. When I laid my hands upon Pastor Santosh, electric power flowed into his body. He shook violently and fell to the ground. Blessed are the hungry! For they shall be filled! During the evening healing meetings, he watched me closely as I gave words of knowledge and prayed for the crowd, and he witnessed many healings, miracles, and deliverances.

Immediately after the conference, he went back to his home village and began applying everything he learned. What was the result? Two children, ages six and seven, who were born blind, were miraculously healed and can now see! Pastor Santosh ministered healing prayer to a fifteen-year-old girl, who suffered from polio and had great difficulty walking with a cane. After prayer, she immediately started running! A 14-year-old girl who was born deaf instantly started hearing! These miracles happened immediately after the impartation prayer and applying proper teaching. Pastor Santosh is a man anointed by the Spirit of God, and every week he shares testimonies of the miraculous works of God that are now a part of his normal life.

Pastor Ankit Sajwan and I were in Pauri Garhwal at a miracle meeting. The second day, he was planning to speak and I was sharing with him how I usually receive words of knowledge in vision form about sick people in the meeting. Pastor Ankit replied that he had never received a word of knowledge in the form of a vision before. I then said, "Do you believe you can receive it now?"

I laid my hands upon him. At that very moment Ankit saw a vision of a woman wearing a pink and green sari, who was trapped inside of a cage. He saw the power of God come down, shattering the cage and setting her free. A few minutes later, he was up on the stage, ready to preach.

Ankit said, "Before I preach, there is a woman here, you are wearing a pink and green sari. Stand up now because God is going to heal you." About 500 people were in the audience, and no one stood up.

Pastor Ankit scanned the crowd and said it again, but no one stood up. After continuing to look, he pointed at a woman who was wearing the pink and green sari. No other woman in the entire meeting was wearing that color combination. She came to the meeting that day because she heard of all the healings, miracles, and deliverances that were taking place. She suffered from epilepsy for many years. As she stood up, the power of God came and healed her.

One last testimony I want to share is about my sister-in-law, Aradhana. Hearing our many amazing testimonies, she became very hungry to understand and experience more of the Holy Spirit, so she went with us to Chandigarh for a training conference and a healing meeting. While praying for the baptism of the Holy Spirit and imparting to the leaders and believers there, Aradhana was also mightily touched and filled with the Spirit.

Following that event, the Holy Spirit began speaking to her about ministering to others. Aradhana went back to her home village and was teaching in her parent's English medium school. In her class, she noticed that one student was partially deaf and was wearing hearing aids. When she saw him, she said quietly to the Holy Spirit, "Holy Spirit, there is a deaf boy here in this class." Then the Holy Spirit replied, "Yes, and what are you going to do about it?"

She stopped teaching and told the children that she was going to pray for the boy. She placed her hands on the boy's ears and was thinking, "Oh, how did Robert pray for the deaf people in Chandigarh?" Not remembering, she just prayed a simple prayer. Instantly, the boy's ears opened and he could hear clearly! The boy's elder brother was brought into the classroom, and he testified that his brother was healed. Then the elder brother asked Aradhana to pray for him, because he had learning disabilities and required special help with his studies. When the class ended, the children went home and told their parents what happened. An elderly lady came to Aradhana, and upon receiving prayer, she was instantly healed of chronic joint pain.

Within just two weeks, the elder brother's learning abilities dramatically improved, and the teachers could see a difference in his progress! Word began to spread, and the local church Aradhana has attended since she was a young girl invited her to come and preach.

Before preaching, the Holy Spirit gave her several words of knowledge. She called out one man's stomach condition, and as she began to pray, the man fell and began to shake strongly. He shook so hard that his glasses fell off. After the shaking stopped, he stood up, completely healed, and all his symptoms had disappeared. Then Aradhana opened the Bible and started to read a verse. The man looked at his Bible without his glasses and could see clearly! He jumped up and shared that testimony, too, that his eyes were supernaturally healed and he could now read the Bible without glasses!

Aradhana is not a pastor or a leader, but just a common believer who the Holy Spirit uses powerfully. The gifts of the Spirit are for all, not just pastors, leaders, and preachers. Everywhere I go I pray for impartation, and I see everyone from new believers to leaders activated in the gifts of the Spirit, and the same works that are happening through my life begin to happen through them.

Practical Application

THE RIVER IS FLOWING

A few years ago, the Lord showed me a vision. In the vision, I saw the earth, and above the earth was heaven on a horizontal plane, shining brightly. There I saw Jesus on the throne in glory. From the throne proceeded a large, strong, gushing river that flowed down toward earth.

Then, the vision zoomed closer to the earth, and many small rivers branched off from the main river that proceeded from Jesus. The smaller rivers flowed from above the earth to each continent. Above each continent, the rivers branched off again into smaller rivers flowing to individual believers scattered across all the nations. Each river flowed up a believer and then suddenly stopped. The river was gushing but would not extend further.

I heard the voice of the Lord, saying, "From the presence of My Son flows a River—a River so rich and full of life. This River can easily satisfy the nations. I desire that My people would honor My Son and perceive the rich waters of life that are freely flowing. You are My gatekeepers, called to minister in the presence of My Spirit."

Upon seeing and hearing this, I immediately knew in my spirit that the gracious river of the Spirit freely flowed to each and every believer upon this planet. The best part was this: there was nothing that could be done to hinder or stop that river's flow from heaven unto us. But, the river would only flow through us as we partnered with Him.

Then, I saw rivers flowing through the believers unto dry and parched land, bringing life, grass, plants and trees. I could feel the heart and passion of the Lord, eagerly desiring the nations to taste and see His goodness.

The river was flowing so strong. His passion was burning so deep. In this revelation, I realized there was nothing that I needed to do to motivate or move God. He was already passionately motivated, and for 2,000 years His river has been flowing. It was ignorance of His passion and of the river that kept the nations in a barren condition.

THE LIES OF RELIGION

> He showed me a river of water of life, clear as crystal, proceeding out of the throne of God and of the Lamb,
>
> — Revelation 22:1

When we read Scripture, as in the verse above, we can easily identify the Father and the Son. The Holy Spirit is also there; He is the river of water of life, beautiful and crystal clear. Receive this deep within your spirit... the river is flowing! There is nothing you can do to make it flow stronger or harder, and there is nothing you can do to stop that river from flowing to you. You can only stop the river from flowing through you, but not to you (John 7:37–39).

This is not so with the religious spirit. The religious spirit is inspired by the devil (1 Timothy 4:1). What is a religious spirit? It is form without power (2 Timothy 3:5), works over relationship, and the Gospel without grace. The religious spirit will always keep you believing you are so close to breakthrough, but you're never able to experience it. It will teach you what you need to do to motivate or move God, and it is centered upon man and his attempts to find and reach God. The religious spirit gift wraps and presents the Law in the decorated paper of the Gospel. It presents grace with conditions. A religious spirit brings death.

If you are like most believers on this planet, you have already eaten from this tree. This is especially dangerous for believers who come from broken families. My childhood was scarred with abandonment, fear, performance, feelings of worthlessness, shame, and guilt.

Remember that the majority of people who come to Christ come from broken backgrounds (Matthew 21:31–32, Luke 7:36–50, 1 Corinthians 1:26–29). They joyfully receive the Gospel, but can easily be lead astray by the rhythms of this religious spirit that beat according to the tempo of their broken past. To the broken and those with unrenewed minds, striving and performance seem perfectly logical. You entered into the kingdom by grace, but now you feel you are required to work very hard not to fail again!

To those of us who longed for revival so long, have prayed innumerable hours, and have fasted countless days, I want to present to you with truth. The River is flowing. Just believe and accept the truth.

Wherever you go, you have the full backing of heaven, a flowing River that is more than a match for any sin, sickness, curse, or demon. Why is this River flowing? Why can you believe with expectancy? Jesus, born under the Law, fulfilled the Law perfectly for us (Galatians 4:4–7), and Jesus prayed that we would receive the Spirit.

> I will pray to the Father, and he will give you another Counselor, that he may be with you forever...
>
> — John 14:16

The River was given to us because Jesus prayed it would happen. Do you believe the Father heard and answered His prayer? I do. Everything required of me for the River to flow was fulfilled by Jesus Himself. To deny that the River is flowing is to deny Jesus's life, death, and resurrection.

A Miracle in a Public Park

Many years ago, I was in Des Moines, Iowa, attending a Global Awakening conference. During prayer, I was overcome by the presence of the Holy Spirit. Shaking and trembling, I fell to the ground. As He always does, the Lord began speaking to me in visions about His passionate compassion for the nations. Grant Braaten, my good friend, was with me on the floor, also being touched by God.

After getting up, I immediately grabbed Grant's hand and, pulling him, said, "Let's go!" Startled, he replied, "Where are we going?" "Outside! Where all the sick and lost people are!" I yelled with passion.

We exited the building and started looking for any "legal targets," such as a cane, hearing aids, crutches, etc. After walking for a while, we reached a park. There were metal benches, trees, and steps leading down to a water fountain.

Suddenly, my eyes landed on a prime target: a lady in her 40s in a motorized wheelchair. Immediately I made a bee line for her. I was excited about the condition I was seeing. When you are in faith, a horrible situation will bring excitement to your heart, because you are convinced of the Greater One who is with you, who can change any impossible situation in a moment of time.

I smiled, "My name is Robert. This is my friend, Grant. I noticed you in this wheelchair, and I would like to pray for you. Can you tell me what is wrong?"

She explained she had degenerative disease in the discs in her lower back. Three of the discs were run down. I asked if I could pray for her. She agreed. I had her lean forward so I could place my hand on her lower back. Grant also laid his hand on her, and we prayed, "Holy Spirit, come. In Jesus's name, we release healing power and presence in her back, now. We command the pain to go now. Be healed."

After a 40-second prayer, I asked her how she felt. "Ahhh... I don't know," She replied. I said, "Well, can you test it? Can you do something that would normally cause you pain?"

She grabbed the armrests of the wheelchair and very slowly began to stand up. Looking at her face, she appeared to be anticipating a strike of pain as she rose up. To her surprise, she stood up straight and began to walk slowly. Then, all of a sudden, without thinking, I yelled out, "Run!" She took off! She ran down the stairs to the fountain, then ran up the stairs toward me! She ran into me and gave me a big hug. As I stared at her face, I saw the biggest smile. She was beaming with joy! I asked her, "How are you feeling?" She confidently replied, "No pain! There is no pain!" This is what happens when we simply perceive that the River is flowing! Jump into the flow!

Hosting His Presence, a Way of Life

Experiencing the Holy Spirit's presence should not be a priority for ministry's sake only, nor a rare occurrence that happens at special conferences. His tangible presence should be our daily reality.

Instead of trying to "be ready" for the moment, we should live a lifestyle of awareness. We don't need to spend hours in prayer, but invite Him to walk with us in our daily lives and be conscious of Him.

When you start your day, set aside 5–20 minutes to just sit in a quiet place and say, "Good morning, Holy Spirit. You are in, with, and on me. Give me the grace to be conscious of Your person and Your presence. I love You. Come, my Love. My soul delights in You. Spirit of grace, Spirit of life, abide with me..."

Speak slowly. Focus upon Him. Soon you will be aware of His presence. It can come to you in many different ways. Physically, you might feel a presence resting on your head, shoulders, arms, hands, and/or chest, as if a sheet was placed upon you. Or, you might feel heat, tingling, electricity, or trembling. Emotionally, you could feel peace, light, joy, and pleasure. You might feel as if you are being embraced, held, and surrounded by Him. You could see visions and hear His voice. It is that easy. It just happens because He is reality, and He is there.

Stay conscious of His person, and just go on with your life. Include Him in your day, and be aware of "legal targets" to pray for. Who are legal targets? Anyone with a headache, body pain, allergies, or sickness. Anyone bound by fear, depression, anxiety, various addictions, or overwhelmed by the struggles of life. You are the representation of the grace of God on this earth! Step out!

HEALING THE SICK

Now I want to give you the very basics about partnering with the Spirit to heal the sick. The first thing I want to say is this: Healing the sick is easy! I travel to areas of the world and train believers from all walks of life to pray for the sick. It is simple, instantaneous, and easy. There was a time when I thought prayer for the sick was the most difficult step of faith! As long as I held to that belief, I saw very, very few people healed. Healing is simple when we (1) understand His grace, and (2) partner with the Holy Spirit.

Before we dive in, let me share with you two testimonies. I was in Punjab, India, training brand new believers about the Holy Spirit and prayer for the sick. Most of them were believers for less than one month and are from Hindu backgrounds. After an exhilarating training, we sent them back to their villages.

One young man was sitting on a brick wall in his village, just chatting with his friend. Suddenly, he heard the voice of the Spirit, saying, "Go into that house. There you will find an old woman who is demonized. Pray for her." He simply responded, walked over to the door, and knocked. After a simple inquiry, he met an elderly lady who was completely deaf. He prayed and commanded the demon to leave. Immediately she hit the floor like a sack of potatoes, and appeared dead. He just stood there, shocked. Within a few minutes she stood up and could hear perfectly!

Another young man was playing Cricket with his friends. During the match, he saw another young man who had a tumorous growth on his neck the size of a walnut. He said, "In Jesus's name I can make that disappear." Startled, the young man said, "How?" "Just let me pray for you in Jesus's name, and you will see." He placed his hand on the growth and prayed. The moment he removed his hand, the tumor was gone!

But many believers think, "What if nothing happens?" Even if nothing happens, you don't lose anything! Think about all the graves full of people who paid untold thousands of dollars to doctors and medical professionals. Do we banish healthcare? No. We just improve it. Let the Holy Spirit teach and train you as you step out in faith. Even if you fail, you will improve over time!

HONORING THE FATHER & SON

Step one is to be convinced of, honor, and respect what the Father and Son already accomplished. The Holy Spirit is not doing a new thing. He always had one agenda, and that is to glorify Jesus (John 16:14). How does He glorify Jesus? He reveals and manifests what Jesus did.

The Father already put upon Jesus every disease that has ever clung to human flesh and every sickness that ever will (Isaiah 53:10). Every pain, sickness, affliction, and disease found its end in Jesus' body. The proper translation from the original Hebrew language in Isaiah 53:10 is this: "...He has made Him sick..." The Father was not sick, nor was there sickness in the storehouses of heaven for Him to use. The Father took all of our diseases and pain and made His own Son sick with them. As far as the Father is concerned, it is a done deal.

Jesus already bore every sickness, pain, and affliction on His own body (Isaiah 53:4; Matthew 8:17). He bore our sickness for us. He didn't suffer to sympathize with us, saying, "I know how bad it is..."

It was substitution. He bore it so that we wouldn't have to. As far as Jesus is concerned, sickness is eradicated.

Ignoring and not believing the accomplished work of the Father and Son is the number one mistake believers make in prayer. All over the world people are petitioning the Father and Son to do what they already did. To petition God for something He has already done is unbelief. If you ask for what you already possess, then you will never receive the answer because of unbelief. Faith simply receives what God has already provided for by grace.

The first step is to be more convinced of the accomplished work of God than the physical manifestation of disease you can see or feel.

I have prayed for thousands of people. I have seen hundreds of miracles and thousands of healings. When I prayed for those people, I never once asked the Father or Son to heal them. Why? Because He already did.

HAND-IN-HAND WITH THE SPIRIT

Next, simply invite the presence, person, and power of the Holy Spirit. Take a moment; don't rush it. Become more aware of Him than the problem you are facing. Tell Him you love Him. Give Him a hug! Say to Him, "Holy Spirit, I don't want to pray without You. Let's have fun together!

Then, simply (1) lay your hand on the afflicted area, (2) release His presence by faith, saying "Holy Spirit, may Your healing presence and power flow here, now," and (3) command the pain, sickness, tumor, devil, etc. to leave: "Pain, you spirit of affliction, come out of this body now!" Then, (4) thank God.

Are you going to thank God because the pain just left? You can. But that is not the focus of thanksgiving. You should thank God because you believe He took it 2,000 years ago on the cross. If you thank God for the momentary "feelings" you experience, you can be tossed into unbelief. What if 20 minutes later the pain comes back? Where will your thanksgiving be? You will probably say, "Oh. I thought I was healed, but I guess not!" But, if you are cross-centered in your conviction, then you always have a reason to thank God, and you won't be moved from faith.

It is as simple as that.

1. Lay your hand for the purpose of releasing presence.

2. Believe His presence is flowing through you and operating with you.

3. Command, command, command! Tell it what to do!

4. Thank God!

Now when the Holy Spirit gives you a word of wisdom, a word of knowledge, or allows you to discern the spirits, then go with it! Remember, prayer is about relationship, not mechanics!

CASTING OUT DEVILS

One of the biggest contrasts from the Bible to our western church is the issue of casting out demons. Everywhere Jesus went, He cast demons out of people, especially in "church" (Mark 1:39)! The devil operates best in confusion and ignorance, and he has succeeded in hiding himself in most congregations!

Often when I travel internationally on flights, I starting chatting with other passengers. I am often asked, "What do you do?" You can imagine the look people give me when I say, "Oh, I cast out devils for a living." Ha!

Do you know the first sign of a believer was the evidence of casting out devils (Mark 16:17)? Confronting and driving out devils should be normal life, not a spooky story we share in charismatic circles.

At least 50% of the healings I have witnessed were from driving out a demon. So, if this is true for the body, then we can reasonably deduce that at least 50% of all emotional, mental, relational, and spiritual illnesses are from demons.

Diagnosing a schizophrenic, raping murderer as demonized but thinking the believer sitting next to you in the pew is normal is the number one mistake believers make. Just as physical diseases have a range of symptoms and severity, so does demonic influence. Just as someone can have a cold, back pain, or acid reflux and appear moderately healthy, in the same way, someone can be influenced or tormented by demons and appear "normal." Just because someone is not vomiting and speaking in various evil voices and his/her eyes are not rolling backwards doesn't mean he/she is not influenced by demons.

Fear, anxiety, resentment, anger, lust, depression, shame, and condemnation are clear signs of the presence of demons. Does every fearful person have a devil? Not necessarily. But, I promise you that more are demonized than you think! Whether a demon needs to be evicted or not, the Gospel commissions us to uproot these evils. As we confront lust, fear, and condemnation, we will often encounter a power lurking within. Just cast it out!

The second biggest mistake believers make is thinking that a Christian cannot be demonized. I am not here to argue about terminology, and honestly, it is not important. Whether the demon is in, on, or around the person, whether influenced, controlled, demonized, or demon-possessed—use whatever terms you want—the point is the person needs help! Don't allow your theology to empower indifference and negligence in your life! Jesus commanded us to cast out devils (Matthew 10:8, 28:20) because He cares about people and wants them to live in freedom. Accept a theology that represents Christ, not a dead church!

IDENTIFYING DEMONIC ACTIVITY

Not every emotion is a devil. Not every sin is caused by demons. Not every evil thought is of Satan, but many are. A simple way to recognize a demon's presence is consistent, reoccurring, negative thoughts, emotions, and desires that won't easily leave, are highly influencing, and, at times, gain temporary control. Also, curses and spiritual hindrances can be devils, such as inability to mentally and emotionally connect with God, inability to focus in prayer, being overcome by sleepiness during prayer and reading the Word, and inability to accept and rejoice in God's promises.

A demon is a spirit being that possesses a soul (mind, emotions, and will), but lacks a body to physically represent itself. A demon projects its soul toward you in the form of thoughts, emotions, and desires. Agreement allows the spirit to "dig in" to your body. Many people don't realize some thoughts, feelings, and desires they are carrying from childhood are not even their own! The first step is to identify and separate the soul of a demon from the soul of the person.

THE BATTLE IS ALREADY WON

In the same manner the Father and Son atoned for all disease, so also they completely defeated the devil and already set us free from His grasp. We must honor and trust their completed work.

The Father has already delivered us from Satan's kingdom (Colossians 1:13). A kingdom represents not just the king, but his entire rule. The Father has already delivered us from Satan's entire rule. Jesus made the devil completely powerless and ineffective (Hebrews 2:14), defeated him and his entire army (Colossians 2:15), and destroyed their works (1 John 3:8).

We must be convinced of the completed work of God more than any manifestation of Satan's kingdom. This is the place of true faith, trust, and rest.

COMMANDING IN HIS PRESENCE

Just as we pray for the sick, in the same manner, we pray for those afflicted by devils. Invite the Holy Spirit, and host His person. The very presence of the Holy Spirit unravels the works of hell. Be more conscious of Him than any demon.

Then, command the (1) manifestation of darkness and the (2) root, the spirit behind the manifestation, to leave the person. For example, if the person is tormented by fear and depression, pray, "Holy Spirit, come. Let the River of Your peace and joy flow here now. I love You, Holy Spirit. Manifest Your presence and power now. In Jesus's name, I speak to fear and depression and to the spirit of fear and depression. You cannot abide in this person any longer. I bind you and forbid your work and presence. In Jesus's name I evict you. Come out! Holy Spirit, now manifest Your presence, peace, and joy. In Jesus's name, River of peace and joy, flow."

If the condition remains or gets worse, just continue to stand in authority and speak firmly, without yelling. Have the person agree with you. Have the person say the same command in an authoritative voice. It is much easier than you think.

Be sure to release the presence of the Holy Spirit after you command the spirit to leave. Let the River of His presence flow through you, filling those areas where darkness once was.

When deliverance takes place, the majority of people will feel a lightness in the body, usually in the chest and abdomen, experience peace, joy, and clarity of mind. Also, the presence of the Lord is easily felt. They may feel an "emptiness" in their body from where the demon left and the heaviness also gone. Sometimes the person feels nothing, but the evidence of freedom is obvious.

CLOSING THOUGHTS

Ministering with the Spirit is fun and a way of life. You don't need to bring shofars or anointing oil with you. You got Him. He is more than enough. Life in the Spirit is simple, satisfying, and fun. We are in a process of learning, and we learn best as we do. Don't be afraid to step out! Rejoice in victories! Allow Him to teach you in failures. Keep the cross of Christ in the center of your heart.

Pray this with me:

Holy Spirit, I boldly ask You to flip my world upside-down with Your passion, compassion, and love for the nations, my neighbors, friends, and family. Burn within me, and make me a flame of fire for Your glory. I want to start a new way of life—a life in which You, Your presence, person, and power is the very center. Holy Spirit, rid me of religion, and let divine relationship burn bright. I surrender to the River. Flow through me to this broken, sick, and hurting world. Satisfy Your passion through me. I love You!

Taking It to the Streets

I want to share a fun adventure I undertook for the Gospel. Let this story expand your perspective on ministry and challenge any "religion" in you!

Kansas City's annual psychic fair was coming up. I had a deep desire to demonstrate the exceeding greatness of the Holy Spirit's power to the lost. The Gospel was not designed to be contained in the walls of the church, but out in the streets. We should not expect the lost to come to our buildings to find answers. Jesus commanded us to go (Matthew 10:7–8, 28:19, Mark 16:15).

Light shines best in the darkest of places. Grace is greater than sin (Romans 5:20). We should not fear evil, sin, or Satan, because Jesus has given us immunity and authority over it all (Luke 10:19).

So, I called the psychic fair coordinator, and every booth was already booked, and there were five people waiting in line for a cancellation! I really wanted to go, so I prayed. Immediately, the Holy Spirit spoke, "You will have a booth at this event."

Within three days of the event, I called the booth coordinator again, and he said, "Very strange you called. We have a booth cancellation today, and no one else is interested in taking it. It's yours." I replied, "Oh, I knew I was going to have a booth, because my Spirit Guide told me two weeks ago!" I told him that I was a channeler who can direct healing energy from my Spirit Guide.

Grant Braaten from Reality House Church joined me. I wore my traditional Indian dress, and on our booth, my bio was written...

> Robert Prakash travels extensively in India, teaching and training how to receive, channel, and release healing energy. Through intimate experience with his Spirit Guide, Robert is clairaudient, clairsentient, and clairvoyant, pin-pointing the roots of various physical, emotional, and spiritual diseases. Having attained master guru status, he is invited to teach, speak, and release energy to thousands in several countries.

DIFFERENT WORDS, SAME MEANING

"Hi! Do you have pain in your body or any physical ailment? We are channelers, and we can channel healing energy into your body and heal you. It is a free service. Are you interested?"

This was our most common welcome to people who came up to our booth or walked by. They usually asked, "How do you actually heal someone?" We replied, "We invite the presence and power of our Spirit Guide and channel His healing energy into people's bodies, usually by laying on of our hands. While channeling energy, I communicate with my Spirit Guide in different languages, since I am fluent in Hindi, Urdu, and Sanskrit."

Some would ask, "It this Reiki?" (Reiki is a Japanese form of channeling energy.) We would reply, "No. We do not channel human energy, but the healing energy of the Transcendent One." Curious, they asked, "How long would this take?" We say, "1–2 minutes." Shocked, they would reply, "That is it!? Wow! That is quick!" With a stern look, I would say,"Yes! Because our Spirit Guide is very powerful."

What is **channeling**? It is releasing the flow of a spirit. Laying on of hands is a foundational teaching (Hebrews 6:1–2) of releasing the presence and power of the Holy Spirit.

What is a **spirit guide**? It is a spirit you personally lean on and seek guidance from. The Holy Spirit is our Spirit Guide (John 16:13).

Transcendent means supreme, surpassing, and exceeding. In a way, transcendent means holy.

Psychic means sensitive to powers of supernatural origin. Can you be psychic in the Holy Spirit? That is exactly what words of knowledge, prophecy, and discerning of spirits are. Walking in the Spirit (Galatians 5:16, 25; Romans 8:4) is being sensitive to—or "psychic in"—the Holy Spirit.

We would pray, "Spirit of Truth, we invite Your presence and power. Healing energy, flow into his/her body now. (Then, I would say in Hindi) In Jesus's name, I command this pain and the source of this pain to be gone."

> For though I was free from all, I brought myself under bondage to all, that I might gain the more. To the Jews, I became as a Jew, that I might gain Jews; to those who are under the law, as under the law, that I might gain those who are under the law; to those who are without law, as without law (not being without law toward God, but under law toward Christ), that I might win those who are without law. To the weak, I became as weak, that I might gain the weak. I have become all things to all men, that I may by all means save some.
>
> — 1 Corinthians 9:19–22

Many believers are too "Christianized" or "religious" to make simple spiritual conversations with unbelievers. But, Apostle Paul was not that way. He didn't worry about words, but conveyed the Gospel message to everyone everywhere. (Paul used the Greek word *theos* for God, which could refer to a number of Greek gods.)

TESTIMONIES

"Holy Crap! Holy Crap!"

A lady named Janet came to our booth after her husband and mother were instantly healed. She had chronic neck and back pain for 20 years. We prayed, "Spirit of Truth, we invite Your presence and power. Healing power, flow into her neck and back now. I command this pain to disappear! Be healed!"

About to collapse, she grabbed my arm to stabilize herself and screamed out, "Holy crap! Holy crap!... HOLY CRAP!" Other people walking by stopped and stared at us. Hands and arms trembling, she sat down in the chair. "All the pain is gone! Holy crap! All my pain is gone!"

After she calmed down, I looked into her eyes and said, "The Spirit we channeled that healed you is the Spirit of Jesus. Jesus loves you, and that is why He healed you. Jesus came to this earth, took all of our negative energies and sins, died in our place for us, and rose from the dead. His death and resurrection forever sealed our union with God. Do you want to believe and trust in Jesus?" With tears steaming from her eyes, she said yes and prayed with me.

"Gifted & Blessed"

Another lady named Sasha was lured into our booth by our free offer to channel energy. She had neck and back pain for 16 years. After channeling energy twice, she was completely healed! She wrote on her testimony sheet, "I felt wonderful, pure energy flowing through my body, and the lower back pain was gone for the first time in 16 years! These guys are gifted and blessed!"

"Forever Grateful"

Karsten was walking by with a wrist brace on. I jumped out of the booth. Grabbing him, I eagerly asked, "Do you have any pain in your wrist!?" Startled by my aggressive nature, he timidly replied,

"Yes. I had multiple injuries to this wrist when I was in gymnastics and other sports. My wrist is in constant pain." I asked, "What would you give your current pain level? 1 to 10?" He stated it was a 9! I had him remove the brace, and I took his wrist into my hands. After releasing healing energy, he said the pain went from his wrist to the back of his shoulder. I then said, "I command this negative entity to leave him now!" Instantly healed! He wrote on the testimony page, "Wrist pain went from a 9 to a 0! Miraculous! Thank you! Forever grateful!"

Total Body Makeover!

Lori (age 45) came to our booth with many needs. She asked healing energy for fibromyalgia, migraines, chronic jaw and neck pain, and an incurable lung disease. She was in a current pain level of 8 out of 10. Laying my hands upon her neck and back, I said, "Spirit of Truth, I invite Your presence and power!" Immediately, the Holy Spirit started to work. I could feel His presence flowing in me and through me. My body, hands, and arms began to tingle and shake as the energy surged. All of her jaw pain, neck pain, and migraine pain disappeared. All the pain in her muscles from fibromyalgia disappeared. Her lungs opened up, and all the wheezing was gone. Every symptom disappeared, and she walked away completely healed!

Deliverance From Demons

We knew sooner or later that we were going to confront a visually manifesting demon. Allie was 41 years of age and came to our booth with two lady friends. She watched as her friends were instantly healed. Being next in line, she said, "I don't have any physical problems, but I am tormented by negative energies." She looked very disturbed, and, like many who came to the fair, she was seeking freedom in the worst place. If the light of Jesus does not shine in their darkness, they will think their darkness is light!

As I invited the Spirit of Truth to come, immediately she trembled and shook and, falling to her knees, her head started bobbing up and down. Her fingers turned claw-like, and she continued to shake. I thought, "Oh! This can turn ugly!" After confronting demons on a normal basis in India, I understood this could cause a huge scene! I knelt down, put my hand on her shoulder, and commanded, "You evil powers, come out of her now in Jesus's name! I forbid you to live in her any longer. Leave her, and come out now!" I motioned Grant to join me. Within two minutes of commanding, the demons left. She stood up normal, with all the signs of deliverance. I looked at her and said, "The Spirit we channel is greater than those evil spirits that were tormenting you. But, they will want to come back. The only person who can keep you free is Jesus. The Spirit we channel is the Spirit of Jesus. Jesus came to this earth 2,000 year ago..." and I preached the entire Gospel to her. With tears in her eyes, she wanted to give her life to Jesus, and she prayed to receive Jesus and the Holy Spirit!

Reiki Master Healed by Jesus

A married couple walked up to our booth, curious about what we do. Jim, a Reiki master, began asking questions. "Are you all Reiki healers?" I replied, "No. We do not do Reiki here. Human energy is far inferior to the energy we channel. We channel the energy of the Transcendent One." Hesitant to humble himself, he finally asked for help with shoulder and knee pain.

We laid our hands on his shoulder and knee and invited the person, presence, and power of the Spirit of Truth. Shocked, he stood up instantly healed! He wrote, "All my pain is now nonexistent!"

His wife, Nancy, was also in pain. Within just seconds of releasing the Holy Spirit's presence, her back and leg pain instantly disappeared. They eagerly wanted to know more about the energy we channel. We took their email address and gave them an audio CD.

Everyone who was healed or touched at our booth was given a free CD. We told them, "This is an audio teaching about who our Spirit Guide is and how you yourself can receive and channel His presence and energy." Everyone joyfully and gratefully took the CD. The CD contained a 36-minute message about Biblical principles, the

Gospel, and my salvation testimony. The CD ends with a prayer to direct their faith and trust to Jesus.

Undeniable Miraculous Improvement

Mimi was a volunteer at the fair, monitoring the entryway to make sure everyone had a ticket. As I was returning from the restroom, I saw her right arm in a sling. I told her to come to our booth for a free healing. She had shoulder surgery forty days prior and was in pain. She stated her pain to be a 9 out of 10.

I released healing energy, but her pain level only slightly lowered. I continued to release healing presence several times, and her pain slowly went down. First to a 7, then a 5, 3, 2, 1, and finally a 0. After all her pain was gone, I asked, "Can you take off your sling and test it out?" She removed it, but still some pain in certain movements remained. I prayed again. The pain lessened, and she had greater range of movement with her shoulder! Though she was not 100%, she was amazed by the immediate, miraculous improvement!

"Am I Going to Have a New Kidney?"

A young lady named Kelsie came to our booth. Upon asking her where she needed healing, she quickly stated many things, "Shoulder pain, knee pain, migraine, sinuses, and kidney!" Because her list was so long, we started with her pain. Instantly, all her shoulder, knee, and migraine pain disappeared. She yelled out, "This is weird! All my pain is gone! No way!" We then asked about the remaining problems. She said, "I have sinus pressure and pain as well." After channeling energy to her sinuses, she felt immediate relief and was even more shocked: "This can't be happening!"

I then asked, "Wasn't there something left?" She said, "Oh, yeah. My kidney. I mean, I only have one kidney." I said, "We can take care of that for you, as well. I saw a boy born with crippled feet healed who never walked, and he is now healed and walking."

She stood there as we laid hands on her lower back. She felt the heat flowing in the place of her absent kidney. In absolute awe, she said,

"Am I going to have a kidney?!" She turned to her friends, "I am going to have a kidney!"

She ran to bring all of her friends and family to our booth, telling them how she was healed completely and that she was going to have a new kidney!

Favor Upon Favor

The coordinator of the psychic fair came to our booth, asking how we were doing. He was shocked at how busy we were and heard about the amazing healings. He asked for healing for his chronic back pain. Instantly, he was healed, too. He was so encouraged, he wanted us to come back next year, invited us to speak on their psychic radio program, and asked us to do a workshop at their monthly psychic events!

We had over 90% success rate for everyone we prayed for! It was ridiculously fun! Over ninety people were instantly, verifiably healed and/or delivered from demons. Several people gave their lives to Jesus, and many seeds were sown.

I didn't feel oppressed by the demonic environment, nor did I fear. I was conscious and attentive of the Holy Spirit. When you are operating in the Spirit, you are on a different and higher spiritual level, where the powers of darkness cannot affect you.

Fall in love with the Holy Spirit, join the adventure, and make history for His glory! He is waiting for you!

Made in the USA
San Bernardino, CA
24 May 2017